Stadium Stories:

Buffalo Bills

Sal Maiorana

INSIDERS' GUIDE®

GUILFORD, CONNECTICUT
AN IMPRINT OF THE GLOBE PEQUOT PRESS

INSIDERS' GUIDE®

Text design: Casey Shain

Cover photos: *front cover:* Thurman Thomas (Buffalo Bills); *back cover:* top, O. J. Simpson *(Buffalo Courier-Express);* bottom, Jack Kemp and Ralph Wilson (Robert L. Smith)

Library of Congress Cataloging-in-Publication Data

Maiorana, Sal, 1962-
    Stadium stories : Buffalo Bills / Sal Maiorana. — 1st ed.
        p. cm. — (Stadium stories series)
    ISBN 0-7627-3743-3
        1. Buffalo Bills (Football team) I. Title. II. Series.

GV956.B83M35 2005
796.332'64'0974797—dc22   2005043409

Manufactured in the United States of America
First Edition/First Printing

Contents

Dedication

This book is dedicated to my parents, Sam and Joan. There is no one that I respect more than my father and mother. They have been a constant source of love and encouragement throughout my life, and if I could impart on my own children even a fraction of the caring and wisdom my father and mother provided me, I will know that Taylor, Holden, and Caroline will be forever enriched.

Acknowledgments

As I have done for every book that I have written, I would like to thank the many sportswriters whose prose and knowledge I borrowed from to conduct research for this project, most notably Leo Roth, Scott Pitoniak, Vic Carucci, Larry Felser, Milt Northrop, Mark Gaughan, Allen Wilson, Bucky Gleason, and Jerry Sullivan.

I would also like to thank the Buffalo Bills, photographer Robert L. Smith, and my alma mater, Buffalo State College, for contributing photographs.

But first and foremost, I would like to thank the people who matter most to me for their continued love and support: my wife Christine, my daughters Taylor and Caroline, and my son Holden. Without you I am merely a sportswriter and author. Because of you I am a husband and a father, and those are the two most important things in a man's life.

Introduction

It was October 1970, a little more than three weeks before my eighth birthday, and my dad decided it was about time he took me to see my first Buffalo Bills game. My dad worked for Carnation, the guys who made, among other things, powdered milk. We'd get the stuff for free, and my mother would cut what we spent for milk—my favorite beverage then and now—in half. She'd mix a half gallon of water with the powdered milk, then add the mixture to a half gallon of whole milk. Voila! One gallon of milk. Truth be told, it was disgusting, but I dutifully drank it. I guess the reward was the occasional use of company football tickets.

Because of a promotion, my dad moved our family from Buffalo to Syracuse in 1967, but with almost all of our extended family and my parents' lifelong friends in Buffalo, our roots remained firmly planted there, and we would spend between twenty and twenty-five weekends a year back in Buffalo. For me that meant staying close to my favorite football team. I can remember watching AFL games on television with my father and my uncles in the late 1960s, not really knowing what was going on and wondering why everyone was always so frustrated. Of course I came to understand that watching the Bills win only fourteen of seventy games between 1967 and 1971 was a perfectly good excuse for their aggravation.

But on that warm, sunny October day, as I sat in an uncomfortable wooden seat in War Memorial Stadium—the old "Rockpile" as everyone in Buffalo called it—it didn't matter to me that the Bills were one of the worst teams in the newly merged

National Football League. Down on that horribly maintained field, basically mud painted green, O. J. Simpson was going to be carrying the ball for the Bills, and Joe Namath was going to be throwing it for the New York Jets. How cool was that?

I remember Dad parking the company car—some sort of station wagon because we always had station wagons growing up—in a lot, then the two of us boarding a city bus that shuttled us over to Jefferson and Best Streets, where War Memorial Stadium was located.

During this, my first exposure to Buffalo's transit system, I remember the din of Bills fans talking about what might take place that day. And while I'm not positive, I'm pretty sure no one predicted the crazy start this game—my first professional football game—would have. New York's Steve Tannen blocked a punt by Paul Maguire—yes, Paul Maguire from the ESPN Sunday night NFL broadcast crew—and ran it back 41 yards for a touchdown. And then on the ensuing kickoff, Simpson muffed the catch but managed to corral the loose ball, then weave his way through the Jets coverage team for a 95-yard touchdown.

Namath countered with a 72-yard touchdown pass to Rich Caster, then came to the sidelines with an apparent wardrobe malfunction. But unlike Janet Jackson at Super Bowl XXXVIII, Broadway Joe wasn't willing to reveal himself. With his team-mates circled around him, Namath dropped his pants to fix what-ever problem he had, and the ladies in the crowd were prevented from getting a free peek at the legs that had become world famous because of his panty hose commercials.

Simpson wound up rushing for 99 yards—his best day as a pro to that point—and his 1-yard touchdown run in the fourth quarter helped the Bills turn a 31–20 deficit into a surprising

34–31 victory. I remember skipping out of the Rockpile holding my dad's hand, thinking all was right in my world that afternoon.

Another event I'll never forget was opening night at palatial Rich Stadium, the new home of the Bills, located in some little suburban town I didn't even know existed called Orchard Park. My dad managed to get the Carnation tickets for the sold-out game, and we were among the 80,020 people who jammed into the new football haven, with its shiny blue aluminum seats, its perfect artificial turf, and its $2 million scoreboard that could actually show replays.

What I remember most about that night was Herb Mulkey of the Washington Redskins christening the stadium by returning the opening kickoff 103 yards for a touchdown. Imagine that. First play in the brand-new stadium, about 60,000 fans on their feet roaring, while the other 20,000 ticketholders were still stuck in traffic trying to get to the game and roaring in a different manner, and the opposing team runs the kickoff back for a touchdown. Talk about a kick in the stomach, but we Bills fans had come to expect the worst in those days.

I left the stadium that night, after the Redskins had beaten the Bills, clutching the commemorative gold coin that everyone in attendance received—a memento I still have to this day. As we sat in a traffic jam that turned what normally would have been a twenty-minute ride home into a two-hour journey, I daydreamed about future games that I might be able to attend, but at that young age, there was no way to know that Rich Stadium—now called Ralph Wilson Stadium—would become such an integral part of my adult life.

By the sixth grade I had taken an interest in writing. And before I entered high school, I had determined that when I grew up I wanted to be a sportswriter, my primary goal being to cover the Bills. I made my dream come true, and since 1990 I have covered the Bills full-time for the *Rochester Democrat and Chronicle*. From my early years as a fan, when I sat in the stands and cheered on the Bills or watched them on television and drove my parents crazy with my passionate screams, right through the last fifteen years, when the press box was my vantage point, I have had a unique connection with this team.

What a ride it was to cover an unprecedented four straight runs to the Super Bowl my first four years on the Bills beat and to chronicle the exploits of a team that won six AFC East Division crowns in an eight-year span.

What a thrill it was to watch players such as Jim Kelly, Thurman Thomas, Andre Reed, Bruce Smith, and Cornelius Bennett, though it wasn't always such a thrill talking with them after they'd had a particularly bad day on the field.

What a pleasure it was to listen to coach Marv Levy, his scholarly words and his usual gentlemanly manner, except on game day when an official would make a call that went against the Bills.

What an honor it was to get to know men such as Kent Hull, Darryl Talley, Don Beebe, Steve Tasker, Frank Reich, Pete Metzelaars, Jim Ritcher, Mark Kelso, Scott Norwood, Henry Jones, Jerry Ostroski, and Ruben Brown, class acts of the highest order who always offered perspective regardless of the final score.

It's been an interesting experience writing this book and compiling my previously published two-volume history of the Bills entitled *Relentless: The Hard-Hitting History of Buffalo Bills Football*. I learned a lot about the men who laid the foundation for this franchise: team owner Ralph Wilson, coach Lou Saban, and players like Jack Kemp, Cookie Gilchrist, Billy Shaw, Tom Sestak, Elbert Dubenion, Mike Stratton, Booker Edgerson, Ron McDole, Al Bemiller, Stew Barber, and Harry Jacobs.

Stadium Stories: Buffalo Bills is my attempt to capture the essence of the Bills franchise, from the ragtag days of the AFL in the 1960s to the twenty-first century, where luxury suites and eight-digit contracts rule the day. In these pages you will read about the good times (four straight AFC championships), the bad times (losing twenty straight to the hated Dolphins), and the men who left an indelible impression on the franchise and the community.

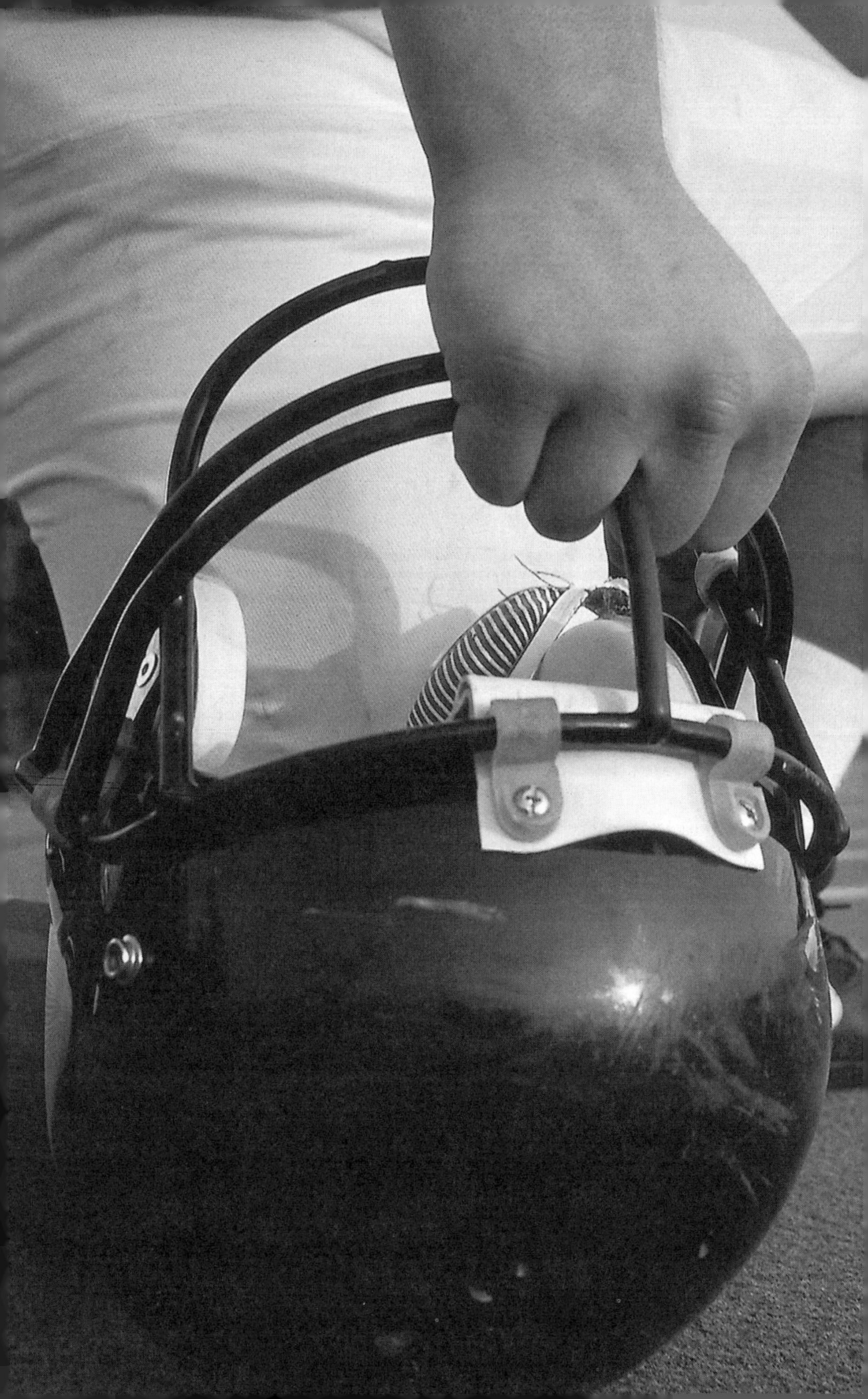

The Foolish Club

It was August 1959, and Ralph C. Wilson Jr. was in Saratoga Springs, New York, for the annual horse-racing meet, rubbing elbows with the other crested-blazer types who descend on the picturesque small town in northeastern New York State every summer. One day, while taking a break from watching the thoroughbreds thunder around the famous track, Wilson came across a particularly intriguing news story in the *New York Times.* "I read where a young man named Lamar Hunt, who had an oil business in Dallas, was starting a new pro football league, and he wanted a franchise in Dallas," Wilson said with a glint in his eyes, recalling the moment that changed his life forever—the moment that ultimately served as the genesis for the birth of the Buffalo Bills.

A lifelong football fan who, along with his father, Ralph Sr., was a minority partner in the ownership group of the National Football League's Detroit Lions, Wilson was enamored with owning his own professional team. But with the syndicate headed by Edwin J. Anderson firmly in control of the Lions, there was little chance that Wilson would ever gain majority interest of his beloved hometown team. And in probing the possibility of expansion in the NFL, Wilson had been told that the league had no intention of growing beyond its twelve-team alignment. "I wanted to own a team, and I inquired about buying an NFL franchise, but there weren't any for sale," said Wilson. "And the NFL wasn't interested in expanding at the time."

Hunt had been told the same thing, but unlike Wilson (who at least had a foot partially in the door via his minority ownership stake in the Lions), Hunt remained on the outside looking in. And he didn't like it. "So he decided to start his own league," Wilson said, cackling at the thought.

Hunt, Wilson, and the other men who were enlisted to purchase franchises and form the American Football League recognized that pro football had cut a deep swath into the domination of fan interest that baseball had once enjoyed in the United States. In the 1950s the NFL's popularity was rising exponentially. It reached a crescendo in 1958, when the championship game at famed Yankee Stadium between the New York

Giants and Baltimore Colts went into overtime before the Johnny Unitas–led Colts prevailed.

Never before had a football game garnered so much attention. It was irrefutable evidence that the time had come for pro football to spread its wings. Sports had become an integral part of the American way of life, and 1959 was a great time to be an American. The country was free from war, free from recession, and Americans were about to enter a new decade with a young, vibrant president, John F. Kennedy, leading the way. There was ample room for more pro football on the sporting landscape, and Hunt, Wilson, and the rest of the owners—who would ultimately be dubbed "The Foolish Club" because everyone thought they were fools for taking on the NFL—knew it.

"I saw the game of professional football becoming very popular," said Wilson, who ponied up the $25,000 franchise fee. "Prior to TV, there were very few people in the country who knew anything about pro football. But then the games started getting on national TV and it started to get popular, although it was always popular with me. In Detroit my friends said, 'You have a franchise in this honky-tonk AFL?' and they laughed at me at cocktail parties. I was a joke."

Who's laughing now? Certainly Wilson. "Best decision I ever made," he said of his investment in the Bills and Buffalo. "It was a big gamble in the early years. There were many times when I didn't think the league was going to fly."

Intrigued by the article in the *Times*, Wilson paid little attention that summer to the racing at Saratoga. Instead, he began to gather information on the viability of Hunt's idea. In his research Wilson found out that Hunt had made contact with fellow Texas millionaire Bud Adams and asked if he'd set up a team in

Who Are These Guys?

It was once written that when Texas oil magnate Lamar Hunt hatched his plan to form a new pro football league that would compete head-to-head with the established NFL, his greatest task would be to find seven other millionaires who were "willing to buy cabins on the Titanic."

As it turned out, it wasn't at all difficult. With pro football gaining in popularity in the 1950s, there were a number of men who wanted to hop aboard for the ride, but the staid NFL repeatedly balked at expansion. So Hunt decided that if the NFL didn't want him in its league, he'd start one of his own. "We hit a market when it was ready to happen, when it was crying out for football," Hunt said. "Unless we made real bad business decisions, we should have been able to make it."

Hunt enlisted Bud Adams (Houston), Barron Hilton (Los Angeles), Bob Howsam (Denver), Billy Sullivan (Boston) Wayne Valley (Oakland), Ralph Wilson (Buffalo), and Harry Wismer (New York) to purchase franchises. It was Valley who came up with the group's moniker "The Foolish Club."

"It was a foolish club," said Wilson. "It was like starting a new automobile company from scratch and bucking Ford and GM. The NFL was powerfully entrenched. We didn't know if this league was going to go. The odds were certainly against it, and everyone was laughing at me."

But they beat the odds. The AFL enjoyed a ten-year run encompassing the entire decade of the 1960s, and its success resulted in a merger with the NFL in time for the 1970 season. Today, thanks to the addition of the AFL franchises, the NFL is the richest, most successful, and most popular sports league in the world.

"The Foolish Club" seated left to right: K.S. "Bud" Adams, Jr. (Houston), Commissioner Joe Foss. Standing left to right: Bill Sullivan (Boston), Cal Kunz (Denver), Ralph Wilson (Buffalo), Lamar Hunt (Dallas), Harry Wismer (New York), Wayne Valley (Oakland), Barron Hilton (San Diego). *Buffalo Bills*

Houston. Barron Hilton, whose father owned the Hilton hotel chain, had been recruited to place a team in Los Angeles. There were also teams proposed for New York, Boston, Denver, and Minneapolis, though that last city backed out and a team was awarded to Oakland, instead. "And I saw that they were interested in establishing a franchise in Miami," Wilson said. "I had a winter home in Miami, I wasn't a total stranger down there, I had been going to Miami since I was a youngster and spending a couple of months in the winter there."

Wilson phoned Hunt to express his interest in financing the Miami franchise. And while Hunt appreciated the call, he warned Wilson that a couple of groups had already begun preliminary planning to tackle the Miami market, so if he wanted to get on board, he'd better get down there. Wilson flew to South Florida and met with the politicians to inform them of his plans and to try to work out a lease agreement for use of the Orange Bowl, Miami's only suitable football venue. To his surprise, Wilson—as well as the other prospective suitors—encountered fierce opposition, not only from political leaders, but also from the University of Miami.

"Number one, Miami had had a team in the old All-America Football Conference [in 1946], and it had failed," Wilson said of the ill-fated league, which also had a team in Buffalo for four years before the league folded in 1949. "They weren't very interested in going into a new, fledgling football league because they had had one bad experience. They said they would rather wait for sometime in the future to get an expansion franchise in the NFL. Secondly, the University of Miami opposed a pro franchise going into the Orange Bowl because it could possibly hurt their attendance. Well, if you couldn't lease the Orange Bowl, you had no place to play in Miami in those days. So I forgot about the whole thing."

But not for long. Within a matter of days, Hunt—recognizing Wilson's vast insurance and trucking money was exactly what his new enterprise needed—called Wilson and told him that with the agreements in seven cities all but finalized, only one more team was needed to form a balanced two-division league. Hunt said he really wanted Wilson involved, and he named five cities that were interested in joining: Buffalo, Louisville, Cincinnati, St. Louis, and Atlanta. Wilson could have his choice as to where to place his franchise.

Originally Wilson told Hunt thanks but no thanks, because he didn't have connections in any of those cities. But the dream of owning his own team kept tugging at Wilson, refusing to let him turn his back on Hunt's overtures. Wilson sought advice from two trusted colleagues: Ed Hayes, who was sports editor of the *Detroit Times*, and Nick Kerbawy, an executive with the Lions.

"I said to both of them, 'If you were goofy enough to go into a new speculative pro football league and buck the established NFL, which of these five cities would you pick?' " Wilson said. "They both said Buffalo. When I asked why, they said that Buffalo had good attendance in the All-America Conference, it was a good football city, an industrial city similar to Detroit on a smaller scale. And Buffalo had been without football for ten years and wanted it back, so that was their choice. I still wasn't very interested. I didn't know anybody in Buffalo, and I had never been to Buffalo. Ed Hayes said he knew the sports editor of the *Buffalo Evening News*, Paul Neville. He said, 'Let me call him and you can go over and see him.' "

Reluctantly, Wilson flew to Buffalo and met with Neville. By the time he left, Wilson had agreed to give the city another shot at pro football. "He was a rabid football fan," Wilson recalled. "He gave me a real sales pitch on how the franchise would do so well here. He told me people had stood in line to buy tickets for a potential NFL franchise [when the AAFC folded and there was talk the NFL would merge with the folding league], and that they were really disappointed they didn't get one.

"He took me out to War Memorial Stadium, which had about 35,000 seats and had been built in the late 1930s. It was a functional stadium, but, oh, the locker room. I don't know if you could even call it a locker room. There were wooden stairs going up to it, and it was so small, you could hardly get the team in there. Sometimes the hot water wouldn't work in the showers. It was an old, dilapidated stadium, but in those days, people were just happy to have a football team. It sufficed for the crowds in the beginning, with a new league and a new team.

"Anyway, I thought about it, so I jokingly said, 'I'll tell you what, Paul, if I should put a franchise in Buffalo, will your paper support me?' He said 'Ralph, we will support you 100 percent.' I said 'Okay, I'll put one over here for three years and we'll see what happens.'" In the Monday, October 17, 1959, edition of the *Buffalo Evening News* a headline read: "Buffalo to Have Team in Pro Football League Next Fall."

And now came the hard part for Wilson and the other owners, building organizations and putting together teams that hardworking Americans would be willing to pay money to watch play. In Buffalo, Wilson hired two respected NFL soldiers to run his operation. Buster Ramsey, the highly successful defensive coordinator of the Lions with whom Wilson was very familiar, was chosen as the head coach, and Dick Gallagher, who had

Ralph Wilson, left, and Bob Lustig
Robert L. Smith Photography

Other Buffalo Pro Teams

Long before the AFL and NFL merged in time for the 1970 season, Buffalo had already played games in the NFL. In 1920 the Buffalo All-Americans established a franchise in the American Professional Football Association, which in 1922 changed its name to the National Football League.

Former Michigan quarterback Tommy Hughitt formed the Buffalo team. He assembled an all-star cast that included Elmer Oliphant of Notre Dame; Ockie Anderson of Colgate; Heinie Miller, Lou Little, and Lud Wray of Penn; Tiny Thornhill of Pittsburgh; and Pat Smith of Michigan. Midway through the year, after Akron and Buffalo had battled to a scoreless tie, the first trade in pro football history occurred when Akron's Bob Nash was sold to Buffalo for $300 and 5 percent of that day's gate receipts.

The All-Americans changed their name to Bisons for the 1924 season, played as the Rangers in 1926, and then as the Bisons until 1929, when waning fan interest and the crash of the stock market brought an end to Buffalo's original entry in the NFL.

Buffalo had a team that played two years in the ill-fated American Football League in 1940 and 1941. That league died when the Japanese attacked Pearl Harbor on December 7, 1941, because there weren't enough players to stock the teams.

After the war the All-America Football Conference began operations in 1946, and Buffalo was a member all four years of its existence. The Bisons, who were 3–10–1 in 1946, then changed their nickname to the Bills. Owner Jim Breuil sponsored a name-the-team contest, and fan Jimmy Dyson, one of several who suggested Bills after the western legend Buffalo Bill Cody, was declared the winner. In the league's last two years, 1948 and 1949, Buffalo played in the AAFC Championship Game, losing both times to the Cleveland Browns.

When the AAFC folded after 1949, the Browns, Baltimore Colts, and San Francisco 49ers were admitted to the NFL, while Buffalo was disbanded. The city would be without pro football for another decade until the American Football League surfaced in 1960.

been Paul Brown's chief assistant with the NFL's Cleveland Browns, was tapped to be the general manager.

Bob Dove and Breezy Reid were hired in January of 1960 to be assistant coaches, Ed Abramoski came aboard in March as trainer, and the coaching staff was completed in May when Harvey Johnson was signed as an assistant coach and given the added duties of director of player personnel.

Finally, there was the matter of finding players who could play. This task proved to be the most difficult, but Dick Gallagher was the perfect man for this job. He was considered a shrewd judge of talent, and at Cleveland he had set up a productive scouting network that continually provided the Browns with impressive new players. Ramsey, on the other hand, was probably not the ideal man for the head-coaching job, though not because he lacked credentials. Ramsey had enjoyed a productive playing career with the Chicago Cardinals in the 1940s, and during his time as defensive coordinator in Detroit, the Lions won three NFL championships. But Ramsey might have been better off staying with the Lions. He was never blessed with patience, and going from an NFL power like the Lions to a ragtag bunch like the Bills pushed Ramsey to his outer limits and, quite often, beyond.

"When Mr. Wilson first contacted me, I was kind of reluctant," Ramsey recalled. "I was making pretty good money for an assistant, and I thought that if I continued to hang on in Detroit, eventually I might get the head-coaching job. But the more I thought about Wilson's offer, the more I liked it. I knew I was going to be taking a big gamble, that there was no guarantee the AFL was going to get off the ground. And I knew it was going to be a hell of a lot of work."

Harvey Johnson, left, and Buster Ramsey
Buffalo Bills

If only he really knew. Casey Stengel coined a famous phrase a couple years later when he asked of his 1962 expansion New York Mets, "Can anybody here play this game?" No doubt Ramsey was thinking the same thing during the team's first training camp on the polo grounds owned by the future co-owner of hockey's Buffalo Sabres, Seymour Knox.

"We really had to scramble," Ramsey recalled. "Hell, it was a miracle we even fielded a team in 1960. Our talent was terrible. We didn't have any scouting department back then. We only had four coaches, so you had to wear a lot of hats. We drafted players, but I also called around to a lot of my friends who were college coaches to get the word out. You literally had guys coming in off the street who had no business being there."

Ramsey spent much of the time that first camp not only teaching players how to do things, but also participating. If he saw that a defensive lineman wasn't mastering a technique, he didn't waste time trying to explain the problem, he'd try to solve it by jumping right into the fray and demonstrating how it was supposed to be done. Without any pads and giving away nearly twenty years, the forty-year-old bear of a man would line up across from the offensive lineman and execute the proper procedure, often driving the unsuspecting player 15 yards downfield. "He'd put his baseball cap on backward, get in his stance, and tell the guy across from him to hit him," said Arch Matos, a linebacker on that original team. "He knocked a few guys on their butts."

"Buster was very dynamic," Wilson said. "When players didn't play well, they were scared of Buster. He'd threaten to beat 'em up, even though he never would."

Richie Lucas, an All-American quarterback from Penn State, was the first player Buffalo drafted. Linebacker Joe Schaffer was the first player the Bills signed. While they and most of the men who wore the Bills uniform that first year didn't pan out, a few did, such as fullback Wray Carlton. He led the Bills in rushing in 1960 with 533 yards. Carlton and wide receiver Elbert Dubenion were the only two players who were still with the club when it won its first AFL championship in 1964. "I look at it as if we were pioneers," Carlton said of being a member of the inaugural team. "We were kind of explorers feeling our way. New guys were coming in every day, and guys were leaving every day. You never felt secure or like you had a job."

Dubenion, who was nicknamed "Golden Wheels" because of his great speed, and who earned a spot on the Bills' Wall of Fame, agreed. "Back then, when the NFL cut a guy, the AFL snatched him up," he said. "You were watching the transactions to see if anybody in your position got cut. If you came in the locker room and saw a guy about your size—uh oh, hard practice today because he may be in my position. It was a little nerve-racking."

The Bills lost their first regular-season game 27–3 to the New York Titans at the Polo Grounds in New York City, then lost their home opener at War Memorial Stadium to the Denver Broncos, 27–21. The first victory came in week 3, when they shut out the Boston Patriots 13–0, but winning did not become habitual that year. The Bills finished with a record of 5–8–1.

After the final game, a 24–7 loss to Lamar Hunt's Dallas Texans, Ramsey summed up the season the only way he knew how: honestly. "I'd like to say that everyone has progressed as much as you'd look for them to in such a long season, but it just isn't true. Against Dallas we had some situations that were just as bad as they were in our first game. This tells a coach one thing:

The personnel just isn't good enough. We'll have something to start with next season. This year we started from absolute scratch. There was no way to evaluate players, one against the other. It took time to find out which players belonged and which players belonged on offense or defense. If we're successful signing our draft choices, we should get the replacements we need in our club. That's the most important thing for our club as I see it. We'll improve ourselves; it's only natural that we will be better off with better players."

The Bills did begin finding better players, and they were better in 1961. The addition of standouts such as Billy Shaw, Stew Barber, Al Bemiller, Art Baker, M. C. Reynolds, and Glenn Bass improved the quality of play, and it began to set the foundation for the great Bills teams of the mid-1960s. However, Ramsey wasn't around long enough to enjoy the fruits of his labor. Wilson fired him after the 1961 season. "I wish I could have hung around a little bit longer because we were just starting to get things headed in the right direction," Ramsey said. "We like to think our cast of characters got the whole thing off the ground. We'd like to think we laid the foundation for what there is today."

A Championship for $100

When the name popped up on the American Football League waiver wire, Bills owner Ralph Wilson and the man he had hired to coach his team in 1962, Lou Saban, couldn't believe their eyes. Jack Kemp? What were the San Diego Chargers thinking by putting Kemp—the quarterback who had led them to back-to-back appearances in the AFL Championship Game—on waivers? Any team could claim him for the whopping price of $100. "I knew that Jack Kemp was a really good quarterback, and we didn't have a quarterback of his caliber," Wilson said. "I had a friend in the league office, and when Sid Gillman put him on waivers over the weekend, I got wind of it. We claimed him."

That transaction became the single most important element to Buffalo's march not only to respectability but also to back-to-back AFL championships in 1964 and 1965.

The level of play had begun to rise in Buffalo after the tortuous and talentless first year. By the time the 1962 season kicked off, the Bills, under the tutelage of Saban, had the look of a team that might be able to challenge fellow Eastern Division rival and two-time AFL champion Houston. In the 1961 draft, general manager Dick Gallagher and scouting director Harvey Johnson had come up with three offensive line studs in guard Billy Shaw, tackle Stew Barber, and center Al Bemiller. In the 1962 draft came linebacker Mike Stratton, defensive end Tom Sestak, and Joe Namath's college roommate at Alabama, safety Ray Abruzzese. Bruising fullback Cookie Gilchrist, who arrived via free agency from the Canadian Football League, gave Buffalo a dynamic offensive run-pass punch, teaming with speedy receiver Elbert Dubenion.

But there remained a gaping hole at quarterback, and the Bills were going nowhere until they fortified that critical position. On a late September day, that fortification came thanks to a simple clerical error out in San Diego.

Kemp had suffered a thumb injury and was unavailable for the Chargers game against Houston. Gillman tried to pull a fast one on the rest of the league by putting Kemp on the injured deferred list—exposing him to waivers—in an effort to create space on the roster that could be used to sign another quarterback for the Oilers game. However, Gillman, who had intended to reclaim Kemp after the game, fouled up the paperwork, leaving Kemp as fair game for the other seven teams. Five clubs put in a claim; because the Bills had the worst record of the five, they were awarded Kemp's services for the paltry sum of $100.

"The missing piece to the puzzle was quarterback," said Wilson, who had watched his team win just 11 of 28 games in its first two AFL seasons, and then saw it start 0–3 in 1962, the last loss a 17–6 debacle against the equally inept New York Titans at War Memorial Stadium. The last defeat brought a torrent of boos and beer cans raining down on the Bills. "When Jack became available, we spent about two seconds deliberating before claiming him. Jack gave us stability and credibility. Our defense was good enough to make us contenders, but you've got to have a quality quarterback, a leader, if you want to win a championship."

For a while it looked like the Bills were going to be requesting a refund on their $100 because Kemp wasn't exactly pleased by his drastic change of address. He had no intention of coming East. "Gillman was absolutely incensed, and so was Kemp," recalled Wilson. "He didn't want to come to Buffalo. It was the last place he wanted to be because he had been born and raised in California. I called Jack on the phone and introduced myself, and I got as cool a reception as you can get. I could tell Jack didn't want to come to the Bills."

Kemp—whose notable political career began in Buffalo when he retired from football in 1969—says his disapproval of the waiver claim had nothing to do with ill will toward Wilson, his team, or the city of Buffalo. "I had a son, Jeff, and I just didn't want to leave my home," said Kemp, who was Bob Dole's vice-presidential running mate in 1996 and who today continues to

Quarterback Jack Kemp and
owner Ralph Wilson
Buffalo Bills

preside over Empower America, a grassroots advocacy group that promotes his conservative ideas. "I had a little business in San Diego and was a resident of San Diego. I was quarterback of the Chargers. And then I woke up one day and found out that I'd been placed on waivers. It had never happened before, at least in my day, that anyone had been picked up like that. But I was not at all upset with Ralph or Buffalo; I just loved San Diego. It was a shock more than anything else."

Kemp was not available to play until the second half of the season due to his thumb ailment. The Bills fell to 0–5 before Saban's new systems began to take hold, and Buffalo went 7–1–1 over its final nine games. Kemp made his debut during a victory over Oakland, directing the only touchdown drive of the game. He then made his first start for the team in a home game against Boston, but that was the only game the Bills lost during the final two months of the season.

Two victories to close out the schedule enabled the Bills to finish above .500 for the first time in team history, and Kemp realized that moving to Buffalo was probably going to be the best move of his career. "It turned out to be a blessing in disguise," he said. "My wife told me that one door closes in your life and another one opens. The door to the Buffalo Bills and politics and Congress really opened up that day when I realized I was going to go to Buffalo to play for Ralph Wilson's team."

With players such as defensive linemen Jim Dunaway and Ron McDole, safety George Saimes, tight end Ernie Warlick, wide receivers Bill Miller and Charley Ferguson, linebacker Harry Jacobs, and quarterback Daryle Lamonica joining the club, there was much anticipation for a breakthrough year in 1963.

Another slow start, this time 0–3–1, had the fans in an uproar, but the Bills regrouped and won seven of their last ten games to tie Boston for first place in the East, necessitating a special one-game playoff to determine San Diego's opponent in the championship game. The game was played at War Memorial Stadium, but the Bills did not take advantage of the home field and were blown out, 26–8.

"That was a real downer, but I can remember Lou and I talking after the game," Kemp said. "I told him, 'You know what, Coach, next year we're going to beat the Pats, and we're going to win the championship, and you and I are going to go off the field on the shoulders of the fans, not to the boos of the fans.' I think it was kind of a vow that I made to work harder and prepare better and get ready for the '64 season."

The Bills had to be cringing when they watched the Chargers dismantle the Patriots 51–10 the following week because they truly felt they were better than Boston, and the championship game rout confirmed those suspicions.

In 1964 not only were they better than Boston, the Bills also were better than everybody in the AFL. Many football experts said the Bills probably could have beaten most NFL teams, perhaps even the 1964 champion Cleveland Browns or Vince Lombardi's dynastic Green Bay Packers. However, the first Super Bowl pitting the winners of the AFL and NFL wasn't contested until after the 1966 season, and that year, with a chance to qualify for that momentous game, the Bills lost the AFL Championship Game to Kansas City, 31–7.

"I've thought about that through the years," Kemp said of a showdown between the Bills and the top NFL teams of the mid-1960s. "It would have been a great experience. I'm not saying we would have beaten them, but it would have been very interesting. I think we could have held our own."

It took all of 12:36 for the Bills to announce to the AFL that they were the team to beat in 1964. During that span in the first quarter of the season opener against Kansas City at War Memorial Stadium, the Bills blitzed the Chiefs for 31 points on their way to a 34–17 victory.

The Bills won their first nine games before a loss to Boston ended the run and nearly tore the team into disrepair. During the Patriots' game the enigmatic Gilchrist became angry with the play calling and refused to reenter the game when told to do so by Saban late in the first half. Two days later Saban angrily cut Gilchrist, the most vital member of the offense.

"Cookie was just a character; he's difficult to describe," Wilson said. "Not his playing abilities, though. He could be an All-Pro today. He and Bronko Nagurski of the Bears were probably the two best fullbacks I ever saw. He only had a high school education, but he could get up and speak extemporaneously on any subject. He could be very, very entertaining. He was smart, but he was hard to control."

Still, the Bills realized that without Gilchrist their chances of winning the championship were greatly reduced. Gilchrist had publicly criticized Kemp in a magazine article earlier that year, saying he preferred the play calling of Lamonica, but it was Kemp who led the charge to get Saban to reinstate Gilchrist. "We were so close to winning the East, and I was afraid that he wasn't going to come back," said All-Pro guard Billy Shaw. "It was selfish on his part, but I would have done anything to help him come back. He didn't have to apologize to me for anything. It was a scary couple of days. I don't know if we could have won it without Cookie."

Cookie Gilchrist had a sometimes
stormy relationship with the Bills.
Buffalo Bills

"I can't remember any time where I completely changed my mind as I did in that particular case," Saban said. "Once we got that squared away there was no question that if we stayed together we could go on and win the whole thing."

Saban said Kemp's and Shaw's impassioned pleas played a role in his decision, but assistant coach Johnny Mazur made the best case for keeping Gilchrist. "John said to me, 'Coach, when have these fellas ever let you down? When have they not done the job? Why don't you reconsider? If they want Cookie, let them be responsible for bringing him back and making him do the job he's capable of doing.' I said, 'That's one hell of an idea.' "

With Gilchrist back in uniform, the Bills won two of their next three games to improve to 11–2, but Boston kept pace in a torrid race. With a 10–2–1 record, the Patriots were in position to break the Bills' hearts again. The season finale was scheduled for Boston's Fenway Park, with the division title on the line.

For much of the year, Saban had played mind games with his quarterbacks as Lamonica played an uncommon amount for a backup. In fact, with Kemp in a slump, Saban started Lamonica the week before against Denver, and the man who later earned the nickname "Mad Bomber" when he played for Oakland helped the Bills to a 30–19 victory.

But Kemp was brought to Buffalo for games just like the Boston showdown. He was a wily veteran who had big-game experience. He knew it, and he made sure Saban knew it. "Before that Boston game I told Saban, 'Coach, if you start me, I guarantee that I'll win this game for you,' " Kemp said. "I don't know why I said it, but I told Saban, 'If you want to win this game, play me.' "

On a snow-covered field, Kemp passed for 286 yards, threw for 1 touchdown, and rushed for 2 other scores. The Bills cruised

"He Could Have Played Today"

On the summer day in 1999 that longtime Bills trainer Eddie Abramoski presented Billy Shaw for induction into the Pro Football Hall of Fame, Abramoski took a look at the graying, rounding man who in the thirty years since his retirement had yet to relinquish the title of greatest offensive linemen in team history and said, "Billy Shaw could have played today."

Laughing over his southern drawl, Shaw shook his head and replied, "I think Abe's stretching the truth a little."

No, he wasn't.

During his playing career, which spanned from 1961 to 1969, Shaw played at about 250 pounds and was solid as a rock without the benefit of weightlifting and off-season conditioning programs. Combine his perfect technique with modern-day training methods, and Shaw would have had no trouble blocking today's defensive linemen and linebackers.

While the great Green Bay Packers guards Fuzzy Thurston and Jerry Kramer received ample attention in the 1960s for their ability to pull out and block on the sweep, neither were any better than Shaw, who toiled in obscurity in Buffalo and the AFL. "We were a very mobile line because we did run the ball quite a bit," Shaw said. "There were straightaway plays, but our forte was pulling and trapping, which was right down my alley. I had a little better feet than normal, so I loved that style."

Unfortunately, the Bills won their two AFL championships before the advent of the Super Bowl. That deprived players like Shaw the opportunity to test themselves against the more-respected NFL.

"Our '64 team was probably as good a team as there was at that time," Shaw said. "I wish there was a Super Bowl then. That was Green Bay's heyday with Kramer and Thurston as the pulling guards, and we played somewhat the same game. We had Cookie [Gilchrist], they had Jim Taylor, we both threw the ball well, and we both had great defenses."

Billy Shaw was inducted into the Pro Football Hall of Fame in 1999.
Buffalo Bills

to a 24–14 victory and headed home brimming with confidence that they would beat the high-octane Chargers the following week at War Memorial Stadium. "The Chargers were favored because they had won in 1963 when they had killed the Pats," Kemp said. "They had Tobin Rote, John Hadl, Lance Alworth, Keith Lincoln, Earl Faison, Ernie Ladd, all my old buddies. But coming into Buffalo, I think they were surprised that we were as tough as we were."

And no Bills player was tougher than linebacker Mike Stratton, who executed one of the greatest tackles in football history that day. The Chargers had scored just 3:11 into the game and, after forcing a Buffalo punt, were poised to score again. However, just as Lincoln got his hands on a short swing pass in the left flat, Stratton came up and leveled him with a vicious hit that broke a few ribs and knocked the star running back out of the game.

The San Diego offense, already hampered with Alworth side-lined by a leg injury, never recovered from Stratton's hit. The Bills scored the final 20 points and won their first championship 20–7 as Gilchrist rushed for 122 yards, Kemp passed for 168, and the defense held San Diego to 179 yards over the final three and one-half quarters.

In the jubilant locker room after the game, Saban asked the assembled press corps, "What do we do for an encore?" Of course he knew the answer to his own question. The Bills were a wonderfully crafted, wonderfully conceived, wonderfully coached team built for the long haul, and nothing less than a second championship was expected.

Most eyes were on the New York Jets in 1965 because they drafted quarterback Joe Namath and lavished him with a record

The Tackle

More than four decades have passed since Bills linebacker Mike Stratton flattened San Diego's Keith Lincoln and turned the tide Buffalo's way in the 1964 AFL Championship Game. But the memory remains fresh in Stratton's mind because people have never forgotten the hit. "I'm really honored that something happened in my life that people can remember for a period of time and associate it with a great group of guys that we had in Buffalo in 1964 and 1965," Stratton said.

When Stratton slammed into Lincoln and broke a couple of his ribs, the Bills were energized for the rest of the game, but Stratton only remembers what he felt after the play was complete: relief. "I haven't always admitted it, but I was scared to death that I wasn't going to get there in time, and Keith was going to catch the ball, give me one look in the eye, juke me, and run on down the field for a touchdown," said Stratton. "That was the fear running through my mind that he would get a chance to catch it and run and me being out there one-on-one and embarrassing myself. I was just trying to get there about the same time the ball did and keep him from running."

Stratton did that, and Chargers coach Sid Gillman could only admiringly say, "That was one of the most beautiful tackles I have ever seen in my life. That is the name of the game."

$400,000 contract, and that was fine with the Bills. They went about their business quietly, and, despite some devastating injuries, they rolled to the division championship. Buffalo's 10–3–1 record was a full five games better than runner-up New York.

The Bills began the season without Gilchrist, who had clearly worn out his welcome in Buffalo and was dealt to Denver for running back Billy Joe, a transaction that wasn't very popular among the players. "Quite honestly I thought it was a mistake when we traded him," cornerback Butch Byrd, a rookie in 1964, said. "I think the Bills management at the time thought it was getting rid of a problem, but we got Billy Joe in a trade for Cookie, and you could see there was a vast difference. The dynamics just weren't there. Cookie did some things that were unconscionable for an athlete. Something inside of him made him think he was being maligned or mistreated and not getting his just due, and he couldn't accept that. That was his flaw, but you had to accept that and look at all the pluses, which far outweighed his minuses."

Their running game already lacking without Gilchrist, the Bills were crippled further on offense when starting receivers Elbert Dubenion and Glenn Bass suffered season-ending knee injuries in back-to-back weeks in the first month of the season. This put pressure on Kemp and the stout Buffalo defense, and both came through with memorable performances. By the end of the year, Kemp had thrown for 2,368 yards and was named the AFL's player of the year by the Associated Press, while the defense held opponents to a league-low 226 points, yielding just 79 yards rushing per game and intercepting 32 passes.

The Bills won their first four games, then they were waxed at home by the Chargers 34–3 in a game San Diego dearly wanted to win. John Hadl, who had taken over at quarterback in place of the retired Tobin Rote, passed for 314 yards and 3 touchdowns, and the San Diego defense revealed that Buffalo's offense minus Gilchrist, Dubenion, and Bass was in trouble.

A Kicker Who Lined Up Crooked

It seemed strange enough that the Bills actually used a 1964 draft pick to select a kicker, some kid out of Cornell by way of Hungary named Pete Gogolak. But then when Gogolak arrived in Buffalo for his first training camp, he was kicking the way a soccer player would, approaching from the side and whipping his leg through the ball.

Prior to Gogolak's arrival in Buffalo, there was no such thing as kicking specialists in pro football. Teams didn't draft kickers or punters because rosters weren't big enough to accommodate them. Instead, coaches spent a good deal of training camp watching running backs, linebackers, defensive backs, or whoever kick balls all over the place, hoping to find anyone who was at least reasonably adept at those fine skills.

But when Bills talent scout Harvey Johnson saw Gogolak kick for the Big Red, he advised Coach Lou Saban that the Bills had to have this kid. Saban nearly spit out his lunch when he heard this, but on further review of Buffalo's horrid placekicking in its first four years, he relented and allowed Johnson to scout Gogolak closer. When Johnson proclaimed that Gogolak "is the greatest kicker I have ever seen," Saban took notice and chose Gogolak in the thirteenth round. The art of placekicking underwent an immediate revolution.

Gogolak was the first soccer-style kicker in either pro league, and soon his style became all the rage. Today, the only place you see a straight-on kicker is in Pop Warner football, and even then there are very few.

Prior to Gogolak's arrival, the Bills kickers made only 26 of 62 field-goal attempts from 1960 to 1963, and they also missed 16 extra points. In the two years Gogolak kicked for the Bills, he made 47 of 75 field goal attempts and 76 of 77 conversions for a total of 217 points.

Gogolak left the Bills after the 1965 season when the NFL's New York Giants offered him a lofty $35,000 contract. He thus became the first player to switch leagues, which in turn opened the floodgates to player bidding wars between the rival leagues. A few months later, in June of 1966, the merger of the AFL and NFL was announced. "I've done two firsts, so I guess I was a trailblazer," Gogolak said with a laugh.

The Bills regrouped and were 8–2 when they flew to San Diego for the rematch, but when it took a Pete Gogolak field goal with 6 seconds left to play to pull out a 20–20 tie, there were whispers among the Buffalo faithful that perhaps the Bills wouldn't be able to defend their title.

It was pure folly. The Bills whipped Houston and Kansas City before losing a meaningless finale at New York, and they returned to the left coast for another championship date with San Diego. This time the explosive Hadl would be at quarterback and the brilliant Alworth was available to play, so the experts concluded that San Diego would outscore Buffalo. Experts? The Chargers didn't score a point, losing 23–0, as Hadl passed for only 140 yards and San Diego had just 12 first downs.

Jim Dunaway blocked a San Diego field goal early in the first quarter, and that was as close as the Chargers would come to scoring the rest of the afternoon. Their deepest penetration would be the Bills 24 yard line.

After a scoreless first quarter, the Bills embarked on a 60-yard drive that culminated in Kemp's 18-yard TD pass to Ernie Warlick. Just 2:30 later, after San Diego failed to move, Byrd blew the game open when he fielded Hadl's punt at his own 26, sprinted to the right sideline, then took off downfield without being touched. The punt return covered 74 yards, still the longest in the team's playoff history, and the Chargers' spirit was clearly broken on that play. With the defense hammering Hadl and company, Buffalo was never threatened. The Bills methodically added three Gogolak field goals in the second half to wrap up the victory.

Gillman summed up the day best when he said, "We lost to an excellent football team. They are a beautiful football team, and beautifully coached. They just beat the hell out of us."

Wilson will never forget an incident that occurred after that game. "They had an elderly man on the field with a cannon, and he fired it whenever the Chargers scored," Wilson said. "Well, this particular day, the Chargers didn't score. I was standing by our bench talking to someone, the players had left the field, and this old man was dragging the cannon back to the tunnel because he hadn't had much use for it that day. He got right in front of our bench, and I guess he was so mad about the outcome of the game, he turned around and pointed the cannon toward our bench and fired it. He was gonna fire that cannon once during that day."

Four decades later, the 1964 championship seems to resonate louder than the 1965 title, probably because it took a gritty win in Boston to qualify for the championship, the championship game was played in Buffalo, and it was highlighted by Stratton's unforgettable tackle. But take it from someone who played a central role in that glorious two-year run, the 1965 title was even better.

"We had a lot of injuries, Cookie had left, and we were filling in a lot of gaps," Kemp recalled. "But we had a great defense again and '65 was, I guess, my best year. I was AP's player of the year. I was honored because I felt like I had to prove that the first championship was not a fluke, so winning it for the second straight time, particularly against the Chargers, was a great thrill. Again, on paper, they looked bigger and tougher and better, yet we overcame all those things, plus all the injuries that we had, to win the championship. That was our greatest accomplishment."

The Original 2,000-Yard Man

In the fall of 1993, a sellout crowd of 79,101 fans stood as one and cheered for the man who was supposed to be forever their hero. On the twentieth anniversary of O. J. Simpson becoming the first running back in NFL history to surpass 2,000 yards rushing in a single season, the Bills reunited many members of that 1973 team for a glorious weekend of reminiscing and celebrating.

The Road to 2,000 Yards

Here's a game-by-game summary of O. J. Simpson's record run to 2,000 yards in 1973:

DATE	OPPONENT	ATT	YDS	TD
9/16	at Patriots	29	250	2
9/23	at Chargers	22	103	1
9/30	vs. NY Jets	24	123	0
10/7	vs. Eagles	27	171	1
10/14	at Colts	22	166	2
10/21	at Dolphins	14	55	0
10/29	vs. Chiefs	39	157	2
11/4	at Saints	20	79	0
11/11	vs. Bengals	20	99	1
11/18	vs. Dolphins	20	120	0
11/25	at Colts	15	124	1
12/2	at Falcons	24	137	0
12/9	vs. Patriots	22	219	1
12/16	at Jets	34	200	1
TOTALS		332	2,003	12

At halftime of the Bills-Colts game, team owner Ralph Wilson stepped to a microphone at midfield and said, "It's a great honor for me to introduce one of the greatest athletes in the history of sports. The great running back, number 32, O. J. Simpson." And with that, Simpson—who in 1985 became the first Bills player inducted into the Pro Football Hall of Fame—

emerged from the tunnel end of the stadium as his old buddies greeted him with high fives and hugs, and the fans sent up a thunderous roar that brought chills to the spines of everyone who was there.

Simpson and most of the players who made up Buffalo's 1973 offensive unit recreated the sweep play Simpson ran late in the season finale against the New York Jets at snowy Shea Stadium, the play that enabled Simpson to cross the unprecedented 2,000-yard threshold. And then the man nicknamed "Juice" addressed the adoring throng by saying, "Maybe in ten years you can bring us back and we can celebrate our thirtieth anniversary along with the tenth anniversary of this world championship Buffalo Bills season."

In theory, what a wonderful idea it was. In reality, what a shame that it never came to pass. The Bills didn't win the Super Bowl after the 1993 season, losing for an unfathomable fourth year in a row in the NFL's championship game. And in 2003 there was no celebration of the thirtieth anniversary of Simpson's 2,003-yard odyssey because Simpson's achievement, as well as his life, is no longer worth celebrating.

Wilson's words rang so true that November day when he called Simpson one of the greatest athletes in history. But the words of sportscaster Bob Costas with regard to Simpson—his one-time colleague at NBC Sports—ring truer today. "You'll never be able to hear O. J. Simpson's name or even watch the great vintage footage of O. J. Simpson as one of the very greatest players who ever lived without thinking of this tragedy," Costas said while being interviewed by ESPN for the cable sports network's award-winning *SportsCentury* series. "But that's the consequence of what happened."

What happened is Nicole Simpson, O. J.'s second wife with whom he had two children, and her friend, Hollywood waiter and aspiring actor Ronald Goldman, were brutally murdered outside Nicole's condominium in Brentwood, California, on the evening of June 12, 1994. Five days later, following a surreal, hours-long car chase through southern California that captivated a nation watching it unfold live on television, Simpson surrendered and was charged with both murders.

Despite an apparent mountain of evidence against him, not the least of which was Simpson's prior record of spousal abuse against Nicole, the Juice squirted free from his pursuers just like he used to do on the football field. Thanks to his highly paid dream team of attorneys, led by Johnnie Cochran, who clearly mesmerized the jury, Simpson was acquitted of the double homicide on October 3, 1995, bringing a bizarre and shocking end to what many called the trial of the century.

Nearly echoing Costas, sportscaster Al Michaels said during a *SportsCentury* interview, "Nobody will ever think of him as a football player again. Clearly what has taken place since 1994 will forever be O. J. Simpson's legacy, and whatever he did in a sporting sense becomes totally secondary."

Still, no examination of Bills' history would be complete without recounting the wondrous performance of Simpson in 1973, when he smashed the great Jim Brown's single-season rushing record and set the new standard for running-back excellence.

Simpson was born and raised in San Francisco, and as a young boy he idolized Brown, the star of the Cleveland Browns. When Cleveland came to play San Francisco at Kezar Stadium in 1962, Brown happened to stop at a soda shop. As he sat down to enjoy a milk shake, three boys approached him. One said,

On this snowy day in 1973, O. J. Simpson became the first NFL player to surpass 2,000 yards rushing in one season. *Buffalo Courier-Express*

"When I'm a pro, I'm gonna break all your records." That boy's name was O. J. Simpson.

Despite Simpson's standout high school career at Galileo High, poor grades scared college recruiters, and he spent two years playing for City College of San Francisco. There he scored a national record 54 touchdowns and improved his grades enough to get dozens of scholarship offers. He accepted the only one he truly wanted, from the University of Southern California.

In 1967 Simpson gained 1,543 yards for the Trojans, including 177 against crosstown rival UCLA. His dramatic 64-yard touchdown run in the fourth quarter against the Bruins clinched the Pacific 8 championship and gave the Trojans the national championship. Against Indiana in the Rose Bowl, Simpson ran for 128 yards and scored both touchdowns in a 14–3 victory.

The next year was even more dynamic, though USC's bid for a second straight national title fell short. Simpson began the season with a 236-yard, 4-touchdown decimation of Minnesota, one of four 200-yard games he would enjoy. By the time he walked off the Los Angeles Coliseum field following a 21–21 tie against Notre Dame in the regular-season finale, Simpson had the Heisman Trophy in his hip pocket.

He closed his college career with a 171-yard effort in a 27–16 loss to Ohio State in the 1969 Rose Bowl, and less than a month later, the American Football League Bills made him the number one overall pick of the common draft, even though Simpson had sent up a warning flag about playing for a team in the AFL. "I just prefer an NFL city," Simpson said. "I'm from an NFL city and I grew up following the NFL. However, if I'm happy financially, I'm happy."

It took quite a while—nearly eight months in fact—before Simpson was financially happy. His representatives battled Bills owner Ralph Wilson fiercely in contract negotiations, and at one point Wilson proclaimed the demands were "outrageous. I'm not sure anyone short of Howard Hughes can handle the package." It wasn't until a month into training camp that Simpson finally agreed to sign his name to a Bills' contract, a four-year, no-cut deal for about $300,000 that included a $100,000 loan and bonus incentive clauses. When Simpson arrived at the Buffalo airport, he was greeted by more than 2,000 excited fans. Mayor Frank Sedita presented him with the key to the city.

Simpson was presented jersey number 36 because his preferred number 32 was already assigned to a player named Gary McDermott, who said he didn't want to give it up. Simpson's presence created some tension in camp because of all the hoopla surrounding the hotshot rookie. Quarterback Jack Kemp, who in 1969 would be playing his final pro season, said, "There's always going to be a little resentment, but no one can resent anybody when they contribute to a team's success, which ultimately puts money in everyone's pocket. There's also no doubt that O. J. adds glamour to the team. He's an attraction, and this is also going to put money in our pockets."

Simpson didn't put much money in the pockets of those woeful 1969 Bills. New coach John Rauch seemed almost put off by the vast attention being paid to Simpson. When he said, "O. J. Simpson doesn't walk on water," it was an ominous sign that Rauch and Simpson weren't going to be a match made in heaven.

"Simpson was not only the greatest player I ever had, he also was the greatest player anyone ever had," said his old USC coach, John McKay. He was certainly the best player Rauch ever had, but Rauch never realized it. That first year, Simpson gained only 697 yards as Rauch stubbornly refused to utilize his most obvious weapon.

In 1970 when the AFL and NFL merged, and Simpson's dream of playing in the NFL became a reality, the dream quickly turned to a nightmare. Though he was able to claim his number 32 jersey when McDermott was released, Simpson gained only 488 yards before suffering a season-ending knee injury in the eighth game.

The 1971 season brought the end of Rauch's miserable tenure as he resigned during training camp. Wilson asked his head talent scout, Harvey Johnson, to coach the team until a replacement could be found, and Johnson endured the worst season in Bills' history, a laughingstock 1–13 record. Simpson carried just 183 times for 742 yards, mainly because the Bills spent almost the entire year in catch-up mode and had to scrap the running game early in most games.

By the end of that third pro season, Simpson was depressed. His career had flatlined playing for the moribund Bills. Once a shooting star during his heyday in college, Simpson was now a meteor crashing to earth. And then it happened. Two days before Christmas of 1971, Simpson received perhaps the greatest present of his life: Wilson hired Lou Saban—who had led the Bills to back-to-back AFL championships in 1964 and 1965—to once again be his head coach. "I couldn't believe how little O. J. had been used," Saban said years later. "Here we had someone with the talent to be the greatest running back ever. And I, for one, intended to use those talents."

Did he ever.

Part of the process of handing Simpson the keys to the car was giving him an engine that worked, meaning the Bills needed to build an offensive line. Saban inherited tackle Donnie Green and center Bruce Jarvis, both of whom were rookie draft picks in 1971, then added guard Reggie McKenzie in the 1972 draft and picked up tackle Dave Foley on waivers from the Jets.

That year, Simpson won the first of his four NFL rushing crowns as he gained 1,251 yards and the Bills improved ever so slightly to 4–9–1. They closed the year with a 21–21 tie against Detroit in the final game played at dilapidated War Memorial Stadium, and a 24–17 upset of the Washington Redskins at RFK Stadium, the same Redskins who a month later would play the Miami Dolphins in Super Bowl VII.

"I don't think he's even scratched the surface yet, I think he can do so many outstanding things," Saban said of Simpson. "Offenses and defenses have to tie themselves around certain players. They have to have a hub, and then one by one the other players become spokes. It makes the unit better because the others want to reach heights, too."

Hmmm.

With two first-round picks in 1973, Saban grabbed guard Joe DeLamielleure and tight end Paul Seymour, thus completing the assemblage of the offensive line. Throughout training camp, Saban tinkered with that unit, and there were many days when things didn't go well. Those six men had a combined nine years of pro experience so the growing pains were, well, painful. The Bills lost all six preseason games, including the inaugural game at shiny new 80,000-seat Rich Stadium, and when the Bills traveled to New England to play the Patriots in the season opener, expectations among the fans in Buffalo were low.

Not so inside the locker room, though. McKenzie, the ebullient leader of the offensive line, told Simpson, "Juice, this season you are going to accomplish something that no other running back has ever done." When Simpson asked what that might be, McKenzie replied, "Two grand. We're going someplace nobody's ever been before."

The Electric Company

The New York Jets public relations department was ready for the crush of reporters who were going to interview O. J. Simpson at Shea Stadium on the afternoon of December 16, 1973, when Simpson was expected to break Jim Brown's all-time single-season rushing record. What the PR guys weren't ready for was Simpson bringing the entire Bills offensive unit into the already cramped room in the bowels of the stadium. "Gentlemen, I want you to meet a few of my friends," Simpson said when he arrived to talk not only about his breaking the immortal Brown's record, but also about his becoming the first running back in NFL history to top 2,000 yards rushing in one season.

Simpson refused to bask in his glory alone, and he introduced each player one by one in order to give them the credit they truly deserved. There would have been no record without the seven-man blocking unit that was dubbed "The Electric Company" because they turned loose the Juice. Tackles Donnie Green and Dave Foley, guards Reggie McKenzie and Joe DeLamielleure, center Mike Montler (who replaced injured Bruce Jarvis midway through the season), and tight end Paul Seymour were, as Simpson said that day, "The cats who did it for me all year."

The Electric Company helped pave the way for O. J. Simpson's record-setting season in 1973. Buffalo Courier-Express

By the time Buffalo's 31–13 season-opening victory over the Patriots was complete, Simpson was exactly one-eighth of the way to reaching McKenzie's lofty goal as he shredded New England for an NFL single-game record 250 yards. Patriots coach Chuck Fairbanks said, "O. J. looked like General Grant going through Richmond. We were helpless. It looked like a track meet out there." And New England linebacker and ex-Bill Edgar Chandler said, "O. J. had more yardage than Secretariat."

Although there had been some terrific performances in 1972, this game was the one that catapulted Simpson to long-awaited NFL stardom, and he knew it. "I knew after that game against New England that I could be the player everyone had predicted I could be," Simpson said.

In week 2 the Bills were pummeled 34–7 in San Diego as Simpson gained 103 yards. Then the offense sputtered in the first regular-season game played at Rich Stadium as the Bills failed to score a touchdown against the New York Jets, yet escaped with a 9–7 win as Simpson gained 123 yards. A 27–26 victory over Philadelphia was marked by a chip-shot 26-yard field goal that Eagles kicker Tom Dempsey missed at the gun. But Simpson had another big day. After watching Juice scamper for 171 yards, Eagles coach Mike McCormack said, "I'm convinced that if you put a hundred people in a small room, he could get out of that room without touching anyone."

Next up were the stout Baltimore Colts, a team the Bills had yet to beat in six tries, including three straight shutout losses, since the AFL-NFL merger. But this was 1973, this was a new Buffalo team, and a new O. J. Simpson. He gained 166 yards and scored on a dazzling 78-yard run as the Bills rolled to a 31–13 victory and improved to 4–1.

Buffalo hadn't been that far above .500 since 1966, and as the Bills flew to Miami to take on the defending Super Bowl champion, the Dolphins, they dared to believe they could run roughshod over Don Shula's No-Name Defense. Not so fast, said the Dolphins. Miami throttled Simpson, holding him to 55 yards before he left with a sprained ankle, and the Dolphins rolled to a 27–6 victory.

Undaunted by that disappointment, the Bills returned home to play for the first time on *Monday Night Football,* and with Frank Gifford, Howard Cosell, and "Dandy Don" Meredith up in the Rich Stadium broadcast booth, Simpson carried an NFL-record 39 times for 157 yards and scored 2 first-quarter touchdowns as Buffalo defeated Kansas City 23–14. Simpson became the first man in history to surpass the 1,000-yard plateau with half a season still left to play, and Cosell was correct in his assessment of Simpson when he called him "the most powerful offensive force in football today."

The national television appearance sent Simpson's popularity soaring, and the debate over whether he could break Brown's single-season rushing record of 1,863 yards—and perhaps crack the 2,000-yard plateau—became one of the hottest topics among NFL fans. With a 5–2 record, the Bills were just a game behind the Dolphins in the race for the AFC East crown. Buffalo was one of the surprise teams in the league.

But quicker than a Simpson sweep around the end, the Bills' playoff dreams were dealt a severe blow over the next three weeks with losses to New Orleans, Cincinnati, and Miami. With 1,322 yards, O. J. was still on pace to break Brown's record, but 2,000 now looked about as out of reach as Buffalo's playoff chances.

O. J. Simpson being led around the corner by guard Joe DeLamielleure.
Buffalo Courier-Express

Wins over Baltimore and Atlanta kept the Bills alive, but with Simpson gaining just 124 and 137 yards, his season total stood at 1,584 yards with two games to go. It was going to take quite a finish for Simpson to reach 2,000—and it was quite a finish that he produced.

Despite running on a snow-covered field in the final home game against New England, Simpson slipped through the Patriots for 219 yards in a 37–13 victory. It was a stunning performance that cast a glaring spotlight on Simpson as he headed to the Big Apple for the season finale at Shea Stadium.

Although the Bills were mathematically still alive in the race for the wild card, their hopes of making it to the playoffs for the first time since 1966 were slim. So Simpson's bid for immortality

Check the Math

When Budd Thalman picked up the ringing telephone in his Orchard Park home late on the evening of December 16, 1973, and heard the man on the other end identify himself as Seymour Siwoff, his heart skipped a beat, or two, or three. Thalman was the Bills first-year public relations director, and he had just orchestrated the press conference of all press conferences when O. J. Simpson and the entire starting offensive team met the media at New York's Shea Stadium after Simpson had become the league's first 2,000-yard rusher.

Siwoff was the head of Elias Sports Bureau, the official statisticians of the NFL, and when he told Thalman that the stat crew working the Bills-Jets game had miscalculated Simpson's yardage total for the day, Thalman nearly fell over in panic. "I'm thinking the NFL's first 2,000-yard man is about to become the NFL's first 1,999-yard man," said Thalman, who had been providing updates on Simpson's yardage total to the Bills bench. Once Simpson surpassed the never-before-reached 2,000-yard mark, coach Lou Saban pulled him from the game, and now Thalman was thinking that Simpson had been yanked before he had actually achieved the milestone.

"I'm thinking of all the people who are going to strangle me," Thalman said. "Juice. Saban. Those big offensive linemen. I'm thinking about calling my real estate agent and the moving company so I can get out of town before this hits the papers."

Fortunately, Siwoff had good news. The stat crew had actually shortchanged Simpson by 2 yards, so instead of the 2,001 total the Bills thought Simpson had finished with, it was actually 2,003. "I felt like a man on death row who had been granted a reprieve," said Thalman.

hogged the headlines all week. On the morning of the game, snowflakes were falling in New York, and Simpson wondered whether he would be able to get the record-breaking yardage. But in the locker room, the men who opened holes all year for Simpson reassured him that everything would be all right. "When the ball is snapped," Foley said, clapping Simpson on the back, "just follow us." Added McKenzie: "Climb right up my back if you have to."

Simpson carried on seven of eight plays on Buffalo's opening possession, gaining 57 yards to set up Jim Braxton's 1-yard TD plunge for a 7–0 lead. On the next series, he took a handoff from quarterback Joe Ferguson and followed McKenzie and DeLamielleure around the left side for a 6-yard gain that vaulted him past Brown. As referee Bob Frederic handed the ball to Simpson, McKenzie came over and said, "Juice, job's not done. We've got lots of work to do." McKenzie wanted 2,000 yards perhaps even more than Simpson did.

O. J. was 90 yards shy of 2,000 at halftime, and the Jets made him work for every yard in the second half. Finally, with about six minutes left to play, Simpson burst through the middle. By the time New York's Phil Wise tackled him 7 yards downfield, the magical mark had been achieved. The game was stopped, Simpson was carried off the field by his teammates, and at that moment he was on top of the world. "Just two years ago I was as low as I could be, so you will never realize just how much this means to me," Simpson said that momentous day.

Turns out Simpson didn't realize how low he really could go.

The Lost Decade

There are days that you remember for your entire life. For me there are a few obvious ones such as the day I got married and, of course, the days my three wonderful children were born. I won't forget the summer day in 1998 when I shot a two-under-par 69 at my home golf club, the first—and still only—time I have broken 70. And during my career as a sportswriter, there have been a number of never-to-be-forgotten highlights: covering the 1995 Ryder Cup matches right here where I live in Rochester, New York; Super Bowl–XXV in Tampa, when Scott Norwood's field-goal attempt sailing wide right was overshadowed only by America's entrance into the Gulf War; and the Bills miraculous, record-breaking, eye-bulging comeback victory over Houston in the 1992 NFL playoffs.

And there's one other day that will forever hold a place in my memory: The gloriously sunny afternoon of September 7, 1980, when, as a college freshman, I sat in Rich Stadium with some of my best friends and watched the Bills—the team I had been following since I was six years old—defeat the hated Dolphins 17–7 to snap an NFL-record twenty-game losing streak to Miami.

Funny, but I'm not the only one who reserves a special place in his memory bank for that day. "That was a great day," said Bills owner Ralph Wilson, who keenly recalls a large portion of the sellout crowd of nearly 80,000 storming the field in celebration, tearing down the goalposts, and trying to present one of the uprights to Wilson as a souvenir. "I remember them passing the upright all the way up to my box. I thought they were going to ram it right through the window. I'll never forget that day."

What struck me then and still strikes me today is the emotional release that took place once the victory was complete. Not so much from the players, many of whom were in high school or even grade school when the losing streak began in October 1970. Only a select few—men such as Joe Ferguson and Reggie McKenzie who had endured, respectively, fourteen and sixteen consecutive losses to the Dolphins—could even begin to comprehend the frustration of the long-suffering fans. But even their glee couldn't compare with what went on inside that stadium and everywhere in western New York in the hours that followed. I'm not sure winning a Super Bowl could feel any better.

Fred Smerlas was on the field that day playing as a second-year nose tackle. Although he had only been a part of the last two losses in the streak—the games in his rookie season of 1979—he recognized what a momentous occasion it was when the Bills ended their misery because he felt the tidal wave of emotion that flooded Buffalo when the clock ticked down to 0:00. "I remember the spirit going into that game," Smerlas said. "We walked out onto that field and it was like the new era had begun. There was no question, no reservation in anyone's heart, that we were going to win that game. It was more like a college atmosphere. The fans were going crazy; we were going crazy. It was an electric atmosphere. When that final gun sounded and we beat

Fans tear down the goalposts after Buffalo's twenty-game losing streak against Miami ended. Buffalo Courier-Express

them, there were no problems in the world that day. It was unbelievable. It was so prideful to stand in the middle of the field and remember that event, knowing you were going to be part of a Buffalo Bills chapter."

Bob Kuechenberg, Miami's rugged offensive guard, had been quoted in the mid-1970s as saying that "Buffalo will never beat Miami as long as I'm playing." On the day when the unthinkable finally occurred, and Buffalo tasted perhaps the sweetest victory in what was then the twenty-year history of the franchise, Kuechenberg (who was still playing for the Dolphins) summed up the feelings of Bills fans everywhere when he said: "A lot of Bills fans felt like they were 0–20. It was something for the city to enjoy. If the shoe was on the other foot, I'd call for work, school, and everything else to be closed tomorrow. The fans endured and they deserve a holiday."

Here is a game-by-game look at the twenty losses.

1970

The last two years of the American Football League were disastrous for the Bills as they went 5–22–1, one of the wins coming the second time they played the Dolphins in 1969, a 28–3 conquest at War Memorial Stadium. Who knew that day that Buffalo wouldn't beat Miami for another decade?

The Dolphins had only been in existence the final four years of the AFL, and their combined record was a woeful 15–39–2, though they were a respectable 3–4–1 against the Bills. However, Don Shula was lured from Baltimore to Miami in 1970, and the Dolphins fortunes changed immediately under the man who would go on to become the winningest head coach in NFL history.

In 1970, the first year of the new, merged NFL, Miami finished second behind the Colts in the AFC East with a 10-4 record and earned a wild-card playoff berth, while the Bills stumbled to a 3–10–1 mark. Two of Buffalo's losses came to Miami, beginning the streak. In mid-October at Buffalo, Miami rolled to a 33–14 victory despite a team-record 348 yards passing by Bills rookie quarterback Dennis Shaw. What doomed the Bills were 6 turnovers—2 Shaw interceptions and 4 fumbles—and O. J. Simpson was held to 35 yards rushing on just 11 attempts. The teams met again in the season finale, a meaningless game because the Dolphins had already wrapped up the wild-card berth, and the Bills were running for the bus that would take them into the off-season. It was never a contest as the Dolphins scored 21 first-quarter points and rolled 45–7.

Embattled Bills coach John Rauch saw his Buffalo record fall to 7–21–1 and there was speculation that he'd be fired. "We've got to get together next year or have no football team," said linebacker Edgar Chandler. "If we had given him a better effort at times, he may have given us a better side of himself. You can't pat a losing team on the back too much. I certainly hope he's back; he has a tremendous knowledge of the game."

1971

Rauch wasn't back in 1971 because he quit in the middle of training camp. He saved himself a lot of grief as the 1–13 Bills endured the worst season in franchise history. "I don't think Vince Lombardi could have done anything with that squad," Wilson recalled. Shaw, who was the NFL's rookie of the year after his promising 1970 season, crashed and burned in 1971. He passed for 12 touchdowns compared with 32 interceptions, the Bills were shut out four times, and their leading scorer was kicker John Leypoldt with 39 points.

In the first game against Miami, the Bills defense actually played well as it limited the Dolphins to four Garo Yepremian field goals in the first half, and the score was only 12–7. But Miami took advantage of Buffalo mistakes in the second half, and its lethal running game tore holes in the Bills defense. By day's end both Larry Csonka and Jim Kiick had rushed for more than 100 yards in a 29–14 victory. "They kept our offense in dry dock," said interim coach Harvey Johnson. "They just took the play away from us. Those two bulls ran over, around, and through our defense."

The teams met again six weeks later, and the Dolphins rushed for 302 yards, including 116 by Mercury Morris in a 34–0 victory. It was Miami's first shutout in team history. Buffalo fell to 0–8 on the season as it contributed 5 turnovers, 3 coming in Miami territory in the first half.

"It seems that each week we find a way to lose," said Simpson, who rushed for 90 yards. "This week it was fumbles. Who knows what it will be next week? Before the season is over, I know we're going to win a few. Sooner or later we're going to stop making the mistakes that have been holding us back. Anyway, with the way we're going, we should get plenty of help in the draft."

1972

Simpson was right in one aspect, and wrong in the other. The Bills won only once that year, but they did get some help in the draft as offensive guard Reggie McKenzie joined the club as a second-round choice out of Michigan.

Miami linebacker Bob Matheson sacks Bills quarterback Dennis Shaw.
Buffalo Courier-Express

McKenzie would go on to be Simpson's "main man" as a pulling guard, and that relationship began budding immediately. Lou Saban, who had coached the Bills to back-to-back AFL championships in 1964 and 1965, was rehired to rescue the franchise, and the Bills made improvement in 1972. They went 4–9–1 and Simpson—finally utilized properly—led the NFL in rushing with 1,251 yards. But Simpson's prowess mattered little in two more losses to a Miami team that became the first in NFL history to win every one of its games, seventeen in a row, on the way to winning Super Bowl VII.

The Bills gave Miami one of its toughest games, though, losing 24–23 in week 6 at the Orange Bowl. Dolphins quarterback Bob Griese had suffered a knee injury the week before, so thirty-eight-year-old backup Earl Morrall made his first start for the Dolphins. Buffalo cornerback Ken Lee picked off a Morrall pass and returned it 16 yards for a touchdown, and the Bills actually led 13–7 at the half before a fumble and a blocked punt set up 10 Miami points in the third quarter. A late Buffalo touchdown left the Bills one point shy.

A few weeks later at War Memorial Stadium, the Bills grabbed a 7–3 first-quarter lead, but the Dolphins wore them down with 254 rushing yards. Morris gained 106 yards in Miami's 30–16 triumph.

1973

This was a magical year for the Bills as Simpson became the first player in NFL history to rush for more than 2,000 yards in a season. However, the Dolphins were unimpressed by the Juice. In the first meeting both teams entered with 4–1 records to sit tied atop the AFC East, but the Dolphins laughed at any comparisons made between them and Buffalo. They held Simpson to 55 yards—his lowest output of the year—in a 27–6 rout at the Orange Bowl, a game in which Buffalo quarterbacks Joe Ferguson and Dennis Shaw combined for 1 net passing yard.

In the rematch in November, Miami's first visit to new Rich Stadium resulted in a 17–0 victory. On this day Simpson achieved one of only two 100-yard rushing performances he had against the Dolphins in his career, gaining 120. It drew the ire of the Dolphins, who believed the Bills primary goal wasn't winning the game but making sure O. J. got his yards. "In our minds Saban gave up the chance to win to get O. J. the 100 yards," said linebacker Nick Buoniconti. "We were laughing at them. We were yelling a lot of profanities, calling them dummies. I said, 'Juice, what's the matter, don't you have any character, don't you want to win the game?' They didn't say anything. It wasn't their fault. It was Saban. To me it was like surrendering, like a capitulation."

Miami defensive tackle Manny Fernandez remembers walking up to McKenzie and saying, "You idiots! Look at the scoreboard!"

1974

Though the Bills just missed making the playoffs in 1973, their 9–5 record was a sign that Saban had the team headed in the right direction, and in 1974 Buffalo qualified for the postseason on the strength of another 9–5 record. The Bills finished two games behind the Dolphins, and naturally, you know why: two more losses to the two-time defending Super Bowl–champion Dolphins.

Zero for the Decade

Here's the Bills record twenty-game losing streak to the Dolphins in the 1970s:

DATE	SITE	SCORE
10/18/70	War Memorial Stadium	14–33
12/20/70	Orange Bowl	7–45
9/26/71	War Memorial Stadium	14–29
11/7/71	Orange Bowl	0–34
10/22/72	Orange Bowl	23–24
11/5/72	War Memorial Stadium	16–30
10/21/73	Orange Bowl	6–27
11/18/73	Rich Stadium	0–17
9/22/74	Rich Stadium	16–24
11/17/74	Orange Bowl	28–35
10/26/75	Rich Stadium	30–35
12/7/75	Orange Bowl	21–31
9/13/76	Rich Stadium	21–30
12/5/76	Orange Bowl	27–45
9/18/77	Rich Stadium	0–13
12/17/77	Orange Bowl	14–31
9/17/78	Orange Bowl	24–31
11/12/78	Rich Stadium	24–25
9/2/79	Rich Stadium	7–9
10/14/79	Orange Bowl	7–17

After a thrilling season-opening victory on *Monday Night Football* over the Oakland Raiders, the Bills lost their ninth in a row to Miami, 24–16. Buffalo turnovers and another dominating ground performance by the Dolphins (176 yards) were the difference. "Buffalo is a good team, they came after us, but once again we proved we're a better team," said Kuechenberg. "Last year, the Bills were ridiculous. They ran even when they were losing, but this year they put the pass in their offense and they've improved. They're going to be good for years to come, but we're still the best."

Two months later at the Orange Bowl, the Bills proved Kuechenberg right: They had improved, and this was the most competitive and exciting game the teams played during the interminable streak.

The teams started the day tied for first in the AFC East at 7–2, but when Buffalo fell behind 14–0 at the half and was still trailing 21–7 when the fourth quarter began, it looked like just another laugher in a long line of laughers. Compounding matters, Ferguson left the game with a badly bruised knee, so his understudy, Gary Marangi, was pressed into duty. But suddenly, less than four minutes into the final period, the game was tied. First, Bills linebacker Dave Washington scooped up a Morris fumble and returned it 42 yards for a touchdown. Then, Marangi threw a 44-yard touchdown pass to J. D. Hill.

Miami drove 81 yards to a go-ahead touchdown on Don Nottingham's run, but the Bills answered with a 71-yard march, capped by Marangi's 5-yard scoring pass to Bob Chandler with 56 seconds remaining. The game was tied again and it looked as if it was headed for overtime. Then again, this being Bills-Dolphins in the 1970s, no such luck. It took the Dolphins just four plays to drive 81 yards to the winning touchdown. Nottingham blasted up the middle the final 23 yards to the end zone with 19 seconds to go, and Miami won, 35–28.

1975

The Bills took a step back and fell to 8–6, though Simpson had a brilliant year while leading the league with 1,817 yards and 23 total touchdowns. Nothing changed in the Miami series, though, as the Dolphins came away with 35–30 and 31–21 victories.

In the first game at Rich Stadium, the Bills jumped to leads of 13–0 and 20–7 in the first half and were still leading 30–21 with less than five minutes to go—one of only two games during the streak in which they held a fourth-quarter lead. It looked as if the drought was going to end at ten. Instead, Bob Griese threw a 5-yard touchdown pass to Jim Mandich with 3:18 left, and after Jake Scott picked off a Ferguson pass on Buffalo's first play after the kickoff, Nottingham plunged across from the 1 yard line for the winning score with 1:25 remaining.

The Bills were skewered for their decision to throw rather than protect the lead, but Saban explained his play call this way: "The score is 30–28, I'm back on my own 12. If they stop me, they can beat me with a field goal or a touchdown. If they stop the running game, we have to punt. We had a tough time running all day, and I felt like if we were going to throw, it should be on first and 10 rather than third and long. This game is brutal, just brutal."

The Bills had begun the season 4–1 and were tied with Miami for first place heading into this game, but the loss deflated them. They won only four of their remaining nine games. Appropriately, their loss to Miami in week 12 officially eliminated them from playoff contention.

The Dolphins raced to a 21–0 first-half lead, but the Bills rallied to within 24–21 and appeared to have a chance to pull the game out with about nine minutes remaining before a botched call by an official killed their hopes. Linebacker John Skorupan recovered what looked like a Morris fumble at Miami's 28 yard line, but the play was erroneously blown dead, and Miami retained possession. On the next play Nottingham broke a 56-yard run to the 1 yard line to set up the clinching scoring run by Norm Bulaich.

1976

Saban quit five games into the season, and Wilson has never forgiven him for it. Nearly three decades have passed and Saban's name has not been added to the Wall of Fame because of Wilson's grudge. Saban's reasons for quitting were unclear, but once he left, the team fell apart. It never won another game, going 0–9 under new coach Jim Ringo to finish a dismal 2–12.

The season opener was a Monday night game at Rich Stadium against the Dolphins, and Simpson was of no help to the Bills. He ended a summer-long contract holdout two days before the game and carried only 5 times for 28 yards. Without their main offensive weapon, the Bills took to the air. Ferguson completed 55- and 58-yard touchdown passes to John Holland and a 12-yarder to Chandler, but it wasn't enough to overcome three missed field goals by Leypoldt—who was waived after the game—and Miami's 25 first downs and 401 yards of total offense.

By the time the teams met again in December, the Bills were on an eight-game losing streak and the once dominant Dolphins were 5–7 and out of the playoffs for the first time since 1969.

Still, nothing changed for Miami against Buffalo as it rolled to a 45–27 victory despite one of Simpson's greatest games.

One week earlier, he had rushed for an NFL record 273 yards in a Thanksgiving Day loss to Detroit. He followed that up with 203 yards in Miami, one of six career 200-yard efforts, but still it was not enough to snap the streak, which was now fourteen.

1977

Losses to Miami served as the perfect bookends to another horrible 3–11 season, Simpson's last in Buffalo. On opening day the Bills defense was superb in limiting the Dolphins to 148 total yards, but 4 turnovers, including a critical fumble on a kickoff, handed a 13–0 victory to Miami. "It was just one of those days, a helluva messed up day out there," said Ringo. "You don't belong in this business if you don't put points up on the scoreboard. The defense played excellent, and it's a shame that we couldn't score when they held Miami down so well. It was just a horrible day."

What else was new against the Dolphins?

In the season finale played on a Saturday at the Orange Bowl, the Dolphins improved to 10–4 and kept their playoff hopes alive with a 31–14 win, but they were eliminated the next day when Baltimore defeated New England to win the AFC East. "I said some years back that the Bills would never beat us while I'm here," said Miami guard Bob Kuechenberg. "I've been right so far."

1978

Chuck Knox took over as head coach in the first year of the NFL's expanded sixteen-game schedule, and he brought instant

The Streak: By the Numbers

13 **The Dolphins average margin of victory**

11 **Times the Dolphins surpassed 30 points**

1 **Times the Bills surpassed 30 points**

7 **Times the Bills were held to a touchdown or less**

2 **100-yard rushing games by O. J. Simpson**

4 **U.S. presidents in office during time of streak**

8 **Games in which the Bills held a lead**

2 **Games in which the Bills held a lead in fourth quarter**

credibility to the organization, but only five wins in the first year. None of those came against Miami, stretching the streak to eighteen and setting a new NFL record for one-team dominance. The old mark had been seventeen straight wins by the Packers over the Chicago Cardinals between 1937 and 1946.

The teams met in week 3, and the Bills were competitive in a 31–24 loss at the Orange Bowl, but running back Delvin Williams—who had been traded to Miami from San Francisco after the 49ers had acquired Simpson from the Bills—slashed his way to 125 yards and a clinching fourth-quarter touchdown. As usual mistakes killed the Bills. Knox, who remained winless as the Bills coach, said, "No excuses, no jinxes, no heat, we just got beat. I don't call a bad snap over the punter's head a jinx or poor tackling and blocking a jinx. Miami's a fine football team, a Super Bowl contender."

In November, Williams tortured the Bills again, this time gaining 144 yards and scoring on runs of 25 and 26 yards as the Dolphins survived a scare and won 25–24 at Rich Stadium. Buffalo was screaming foul play at the end of this one, claiming poor officiating robbed it of a chance to win. Down 25–24 with 1:42 left, the Bills had a second and 6 at their own 46 yard line, and it looked as if Roland Hooks made a reception at Miami's 25. But the officials ruled that Hooks trapped the ball, and two plays later Buffalo turned over the ball on downs. "What's happening I think has a lot to do with the Buffalo Bills not being a good team," said Bob Chandler. "The Bills aren't going to achieve parity out there in officiating until they're respected as a football team. It's unbelievable. More calls go against us than for us."

Kuechenberg again rubbed salt in Buffalo's wound, saying, "Well, that's number eighteen. You can't say a Buffalo-Miami game is boring. We've had some of our sweetest victories against the Bills. We take a lot of pride in having never lost to them for so long."

1979

The closest the Bills ever came to beating Miami in the 1970s came in the 1979 season opener at Rich Stadium. It was a miserably played game on offense, particularly by the Bills, who made just 5 first downs and gained a mere 121 yards. But thanks to a 76-yard punt return for a touchdown by Charles Romes, Buffalo held a 7–3 lead in the fourth quarter before Larry Csonka—back with Miami after a four-year hiatus—put the Dolphins ahead 9–7 with a short touchdown run with 6:29 left to play.

However, when Keith Moody returned a punt 28 yards to Miami's 35 yard line, the Bills were in position to pull off the upset. They advanced to the 17 before calling on kicker Tom Dempsey to win it on the final play. With the sellout crowd in a frenzy, expecting the streak to come to an end, Dempsey shanked his kick to the right. Miami escaped victorious once again.

Miami's twentieth, and last, victory in the streak came on October 14, 1979, at the Orange Bowl, a 17–7 conquest as the Bills gained just 178 yards and made another critical mistake by allowing Tony Nathan to score on an 86-yard punt return.

Twenty straight losses to one team. Almost unfathomable.

And while the Bills eventually turned the tables on the Dolphins, especially during the tenure of Marv Levy, when they won eighteen of twenty-six games (including a perfect 3–0 in the postseason), the fans have never forgotten the 0–20 embarrassment that was the 1970s. To which Manny Fernandez, the long-time Dolphins defensive tackle, had this to say: "Get over it. They had their chance to win four Super Bowls and lost them all. Congratulations. I wasn't surprised. Any team that can lose twenty times in a row to one team can lose four straight Super Bowls."

Is there any wonder why Bills fans hate the Dolphins so much?

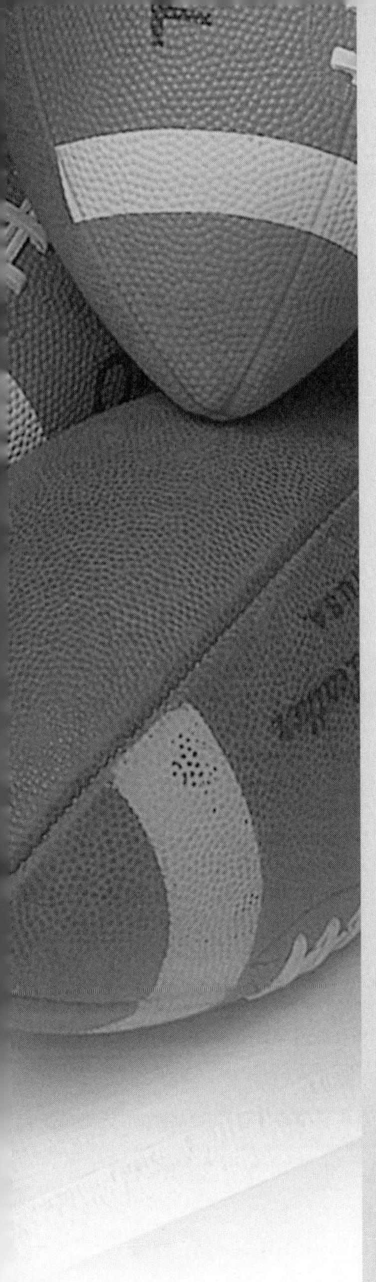

Talkin' Proud in 1980

*Buffalo's got a spirit, talkin'
proud, talkin' proud;
Listen up, and you'll hear it,
talkin' proud, talkin' proud;
The good nights that you share,
with nice people who care,
It's time to tell them all we're up
and standin' tall.
Buffalo's got a spirit . . .*

Oh, you get the drift, because anyone who was living in Buffalo in 1980 knows the song "Talkin' Proud." It was the Buffalo Chamber of Commerce's snappy jingle that was the focal point of a marketing campaign to boost the spirits of the citizens of a downtrodden city, imploring them to stand up and be proud of Buffalo despite all its problems.

And Buffalo certainly had its share of problems as the Ronald Reagan presidency commenced. Quite simply, the 1970s were an awful time in western New York, and not just because the Bills were one of the worst teams in the National Football League for much of the decade. Buffalo was rapidly becoming an industrial wasteland as the once thriving steel mills that employed thousands of workers were shutting down, and the area's unemployment rates were rocketing out of control, leaving the economy in a shambles.

The historic Blizzard of 1977 paralyzed the city for more than two weeks in January, and the clean-up efforts spawned widespread greedy corruption. And in 1978 word came that chemical waste dumped and buried in the Love Canal section of nearby Niagara Falls was percolating to the surface, creating enormous health risks to the inhabitants of the area. It became one of the most appalling environmental tragedies in American history, summarized by a Love Canal resident who put a sign on his front lawn that read: GIVE ME LIBERTY. I'VE ALREADY GOT DEATH. Finally, in 1979 construction began on the downtown light-rail rapid transit system. In the process it ruined several downtown businesses and became a financial hardship to taxpayers.

So to recap: high jobless rate, businesses closing, too much snow, poisonous air, and a bad, bad football team playing at half-empty Rich Stadium on autumn afternoons. Is it any wonder that western New York was a national joke, Johnny Carson's favorite target during his nightly monologue, and a place that was considered one of the most undesirable in which to live in the United States?

Buffalo desperately needed something positive to happen, and it was the Bills—and that little "Talkin' Proud" ditty—that gave Buffalonians the shot in the arm they needed.

In 1980 the Talkin' Proud campaign made people realize that there was plenty to like about Buffalo, particularly that it was a pleasant community, the City of Good Neighbors. There really were "the good nights that you share with nice people who care." Damn the outsiders from the big cities who looked down on Buffalo. Folks from Attica to Angola and all points in between were Talkin' Proud.

And in 1980, the third year of the Chuck Knox coaching era, the Bills gave the city a tangible reason to puff out its collective chest and pound proudly. After four consecutive losing seasons and a combined record of 51–91–2 in the 1970s, including an embarrassing twenty straight losses to Miami, the Bills put together a memorable joyride of a season. They won eleven games, made the playoffs for just the second time since 1966, and in the process made a magical connection with their loyal fans.

"The fans were picking up on the pride that we were developing, and it was really one hand feeding the other," said Jerry Butler, Buffalo's star receiver at that time. "We felt the energy coming from the crowd, and the energy was coming from the things we were able to do. It was an even trade-off and it was great. Buffalo has some of the greatest fans in the world, and I was very fortunate to be able to have been there at that time."

Knox was the key to the team's resurgence. After winning his fifth straight NFC West divisional crown as coach of the Los

Angeles Rams in 1977, giving him a sparkling career record of 54–15–1, Knox was looking for a new challenge. Buffalo sure fit the bill. "Ralph Wilson came out and visited with me and told me what he wanted to do," Knox recalled. "The Bills job appealed to me because they had won like three or four games over a two-year period, and I felt like we could go in there and turn the program around. We turned that thing around in 1980 with the Talkin' Proud campaign and winning and all of that."

The Bills went 5–11 in Knox's first year in 1978, then began making strides in 1979 when Butler, nose tackle Fred Smerlas, and linebacker Jim Haslett were drafted. The team was 7–6 in December and in the playoff hunt until a three-game, season-ending losing streak. Still, it was obvious the Bills had turned the corner as Knox brought respectability and a winning attitude to the organization. They had escaped the abyss, and the dawn of a new decade promised excitement in Orchard Park.

Knox recognized that defense was the priority when he came to town, and his first move was to switch from the traditional 4–3 alignment to the 3–4 that had become all the rage in the late 1970s. After some growing pains in 1978, the Bills allowed the eighth-fewest points (279) in the NFL in 1979 and were number two in pass defense.

Heading into 1980 the defense was set. Now what about that offense? In 1978, not knowing what to make of Joe Ferguson, Knox slapped handcuffs on his quarterback and relied on a running game led by rookie Terry Miller. In 1979 Knox showed more faith in Ferguson's abilities as a passer and allowed him more freedom. Ferguson responded with a career-high 3,572 yards, eighth-best in the league thanks in large part to the exploits of Butler and Frank Lewis.

There was another reason for Knox's willingness to turn Ferguson loose. With Miller mysteriously flaming out, the running game became nonexistent. Miller, the fifth overall choice in the 1978 draft, had shown promise as a rookie with 1,060 yards, but in 1979 he gained just 484 yards. Curtis Brown was a complementary player but certainly not a headliner, and Roland Hooks was more useful as a third-down pass-catching back, so the Bills had issues with their ground attack. For Knox, a man nicknamed "Ground Chuck" because of his preference for the running game, this was troublesome.

Following a season-ending 28–0 whipping at the hands of a Pittsburgh Steelers team that was one month away from winning its fourth Super Bowl in five years, Ferguson did not mince words when asked to pinpoint why the offense struggled. "We've got to get the running game going next year," he said. "It caught up with us the second half of the season. If a team finds out you can't run the ball, there are a lot of things they can do to completely shut off the pass. It made the last three games of the season miserable."

The Bills needed a ballcarrier, and thanks to O. J. Simpson, the greatest runner in team history, they got one in the 1980 draft. One of Knox's first moves upon taking the Buffalo job was to trade Simpson to San Francisco in exchange for five draft choices. With one of those acquired picks, a second-rounder in 1980, Knox grabbed Auburn's Joe Cribbs. "Joe's a special kid," Knox said of Cribbs, who left Auburn as the school's all-time leading rusher. "You can see it when he runs. He has what I call a little wiggle in his wobble. He does a little juking."

In addition to Cribbs, Buffalo drafted offensive lineman Jim Ritcher and tight end Mark Brammer. Plus, Knox signed wily veterans such as linebacker Phil Villapiano, offensive lineman

Conrad Dobler, wide receiver Ron Jessie, and fullback Roosevelt Leaks to join Ferguson, Lewis, Lou Piccone, and Reggie McKenzie in providing leadership and stability for a young team.

Training camp included some anxious moments as the holdouts of veterans Joe DeLamielleure and Sherman White disrupted preparation. Each missed the entire summer and did not join the team until the week of the season opener against Miami. In DeLamielleure's case, he was with the team only two days. One of the original members of the Electric Company line that blocked for Simpson, DeLamielleure—who only a few weeks earlier had been named by the NFL to its all-decade team of the 1970s—had been demanding a trade since the end of the 1979 season. He was finally granted his wish as he was dealt to Cleveland. "I'm not relieved at all," Knox said the day the trade was made. "What joy can you have from it? What we wanted to do was get it settled so we could start getting ready for Miami."

Ah, Miami.

How appropriate that it was the Dolphins who were scheduled to kick off the 1980 season in Buffalo. The Dolphins who had beaten Buffalo twenty consecutive times. The Dolphins who had played a role in turning Buffalo into a laughingstock in the 1970s.

Oh, what a day that was when the hex against Miami was finally ended, the demons officially exorcised as the Bills prevailed, 17–7. "What a drought that was," said backup defensive tackle Mike Kadish, who began his career in Miami but had played in Buffalo since 1972 and endured heartbreak after heartbreak against the Dolphins. "When the game was over, Buffalo, including the Bills, stayed up late that night."

Ritcher was playing his first NFL game that day, and the memory of what transpired has never faded. "The people swarmed out on the field, tore the goalposts down, and went wild," he recalled. "I remember thinking, 'Wow, this is only the first game of the season. This is really something.' It was all too new for me to understand, but I remember it meant a lot to the other guys who were here then. I remember feeling the pressure of that game and the emotion of that win. For so many guys, that was a huge game."

In his NFL debut Cribbs rushed for 60 yards, caught 9 passes for 71 yards, and scored the clinching touchdown with 2:02 left to play. Afterward, he made a comment that symbolized the new attitude in Buffalo. "The way the crowd was yelling, they really picked you up, but what made it different is that they reacted like they had won the game themselves," he said. "Hey, I'm 1–0 in the NFL, and I've never lost to Miami."

The following week, the Bills defeated the New York Jets 20–10 on the day the organization retired Simpson's number 32 and made him the first member of its new Wall of Fame. "We're 2–0, and I think people will start looking our way now," said Ferguson, who passed for 207 yards. "Phil Villapiano and Conrad Dobler talked at the team meeting, and they stressed pride. We're developing pride here, which we'd been lacking. The only way you get it is by winning."

Over the next two weeks, Dobler and Villapiano enjoyed sweet revenge against the teams that had recently dumped them. First up were the New Orleans Saints, who had traded Dobler to Buffalo. Knox asked Dobler for a detailed scouting report of his former team. In Dobler's book, *Don't Call Me Dirty*, he wrote, "I didn't hesitate one second before giving him everything I knew, right down to what [New Orleans coach] Dick Nolan ate for breakfast."

The Bills ripped the Saints 35–26 as the offense produced a season-best 410 yards. Louisiana native Ferguson passed for 292 yards and 3 touchdowns and became the Bills all-time passing yardage leader that afternoon.

Back home, the Bills came to meet the big, bad Raiders, and now it was Villapiano's turn to play head scout. "I was in every meeting of the offense and defense that week," said Villapiano. "They didn't even care if I went to the linebacker meeting. I was just going around helping defensive linemen with how they block and different calls. We knew more about the Raiders than the Raiders knew about themselves for that game. So that was pretty cool when we beat them that day. It made me feel great." The final was 24–7 as the defense forced 5 Oakland turnovers and held the Raiders to 179 total yards. Cribbs gained 126 all-purpose yards and scored 2 touchdowns.

Four weeks into the season and only three NFL teams were 4–0. Two of them, Buffalo and San Diego, were scheduled to play each other in week 5.

The Chargers were an offensive machine led by Dan Fouts, Chuck Muncie, John Jefferson, Charlie Joiner, and Kellen Winslow, but they hadn't seen a defense like Buffalo's yet. San Diego bolted to a 24–12 lead in the third quarter when backup safety Rod Kush—playing because starter Jeff Nixon had suffered a knee injury—tackled San Diego punter Rick Partridge before he could get a kick off at his own 16. That set up Ferguson's 9-yard touchdown pass to Brammer on a fourth-down play that pulled the Bills within 24–19.

In the fourth quarter Haslett picked off a Fouts pass (one of four San Diego turnovers) and returned it to the 21 yard line of the Chargers. That set up Cribbs's 3-yard touchdown run for a

26–24 victory. Because the Detroit Lions lost earlier in the day, the Bills flew back home as the NFL's only unbeaten team. Brammer will never forget what happened when the plane landed well after midnight. "I remember coming back from San Diego, and of course we had gotten back very late at night and I remember there being 4,000 or 5,000 people at the airport waiting for us," he said. "I think that flabbergasted the whole team. There was a huge amount of excitement because of that."

"Buffalo's Going to the Super Bowl"

Defensive end Ken "Baby" Johnson played six years for the Bills, but nothing he ever did on the field was as memorable as the jingle he penned early in the 1980 season that became the team's rally song. "Isiah Robertson would always egg us on and say, 'Who's got the word for the day,' " wide receiver Jerry Butler remembered. "We'd have our team meeting on Friday, just the players, and he kind of coined that phrase. So one day it was Baby Johnson's turn for the word, and he pulled out this piece of paper and said, 'I've got a song for you.' So everybody was all into it, and he's up there saying, 'Quiet down, quiet down.'

"So then he starts in with 'I-I-I got a feeling; I-I-I got a feeling; Buffalo's going to the Super Bowl.' We were laughing at first, but it kind of just stuck, and pretty soon everybody was singing the chorus. As the year went on, this whole thing got everybody riled up, and we really started taking pride in that little song. After we'd win a game, we'd start singing. It was amazing that it unified a team in that regard. We jelled as a team, you really felt the camaraderie on the football field."

The excitement diminished slightly the next two weeks when back-to-back losses to the Baltimore Colts and Dolphins slowed the charge. The 17–14 defeat in Miami was particularly galling as all 17 Miami points were set up by Cribbs's fumbles, and Buffalo lost at the Orange Bowl for the twelfth consecutive time.

By falling to 5–2, the Bills dropped a game behind red-hot New England in the AFC East race, but in a nifty scheduling break, the Patriots were next up for the Bills at Rich Stadium. With the winds whipping consistently at 30 miles per hour, the Bills defense throttled quarterback Steve Grogan and company, limiting the Patriots to 8 first downs and 148 yards of offense. In Buffalo's convincing 31–13 victory, Cribbs bounced back from his horrific day in Miami and enjoyed the first 100-yard rushing game of his career while scoring twice. Frank Lewis added a pair of touchdown catches from Ferguson. "There is enough evidence to state we are making progress in our ambitions to become a competitive team, but eight games do not make a season," said Knox.

Knox knew that even though his young team had terrific veteran leadership, there were going to be potholes along the road to the playoffs, and there was a big one in Orchard Park in week 9. Atlanta came to town, fell behind 14–0, then scored twice in the final 41 seconds of the first half on its way to 30 unanswered points in a 30–14 victory over the shell-shocked Bills.

There was another collapse at New York's Shea Stadium as the Bills raced out to a 17–0 lead and were up 24–10 in the fourth quarter before the Jets rallied to tie it with 4:10 remaining. But this time the Bills regrouped and pulled off one of their most exciting victories in recent years, further proof that there was something special in the air in 1980.

After an exchange of punts, Buffalo took over at New York's 48 yard line with less than 30 seconds to go. Ferguson hit Brammer with a 17-yard pass and called his final timeout with 12 seconds remaining. Knox thought about a field goal, but 48 yards on a soggy grass field was a bit much for Nick Mike-Mayer. Another option was a quick sideline pass to give Mike-Mayer a more reasonable attempt. Lastly, Knox thought about throwing it into the end zone to Frank Lewis.

Knox chose the last option, Ferguson threw a perfect pass, and Lewis beat his man cleanly to make the catch. The Bills were 31–24 victors. "I'm glad it all happened like this," said Dobler. "This will be a great learning experience for everyone. Unless you do it, you don't know it can be done. All these young people here now know the game isn't over until the final gun."

A defensive masterpiece against Cincinnati resulted in a 14–0 victory, and then the biggest test of the season came the weekend before Thanksgiving, when the two-time defending Super Bowl–champion Steelers and about 30,000 of their black-and-gold clad fans invaded Rich Stadium.

This was the day the "Talkin' Proud" song made its debut at the stadium. Every time the Bills scored, it blared over the public-address system as the fans—at least those cheering for Buffalo—sang in celebration. They did this four times, after each of the Bills' touchdowns in a shocking 28–13 victory that officially stamped Buffalo as a playoff contender.

"This team can go the distance," said Smerlas. "There's nothing this team can't do. We gave two games away and had one bad game. We could easily be 11–1. As it is, we're 9–3 and we're smoking. This team beat San Diego, Oakland, New England, and Pittsburgh. Who's left to beat?"

Well, the Colts, but that didn't happen. Baltimore completed a season sweep of Buffalo with a 28–24 victory, though the pain was dulled by the fact that New England fell to San Francisco, enabling the Bills to maintain their one-game lead in the AFC East.

Perhaps the most enduring image of the year occurred the first weekend of December, when the Bills beat Knox's old team, the Rams, 10–7 on an overtime field goal by Mike-Mayer. The raucous sellout crowd demanded a curtain call from the Bills—perhaps the first in NFL history—and the team complied. First Mike-Mayer trotted back onto the field, then most of his teammates joined him. They proceeded to dance and drink with the fans who stormed the field while "Talkin' Proud" blared repeatedly.

"The fans in Buffalo were great; they were the greatest," said defensive end Scott Hutchinson. "They just rallied around you, especially if you were winning. But even if you were losing, they were there. It was exciting to see them, and I think it actually changed the whole city of Buffalo. I think from there on, Buffalo actually started improving and everybody had a better disposition about the way of life up there because the Bills started winning."

The Bills had a chance to clinch the AFC East the following week at New England, but the Patriots kept alive their hopes with a 24–2 pasting. Even more disturbing than the loss was the fact that Ferguson was knocked out of the game with a sprained ankle, an injury that would haunt the Bills a few weeks later.

The Bills flew out to San Francisco for their season finale against the up-and-coming, soon-to-be-dynastic 49ers of head coach Bill Walsh and quarterback Joe Montana. Before kickoff on the West Coast, they learned that New England had beaten New Orleans, and because the Patriots had a tiebreaker advan-

Joe Ferguson's Ups and Downs

During his twelve-year career in Buffalo, there were days when Joe Ferguson was so good you half expected the folks in Canton, Ohio, to start carving his Hall of Fame bust right on the spot. And then there were days when Ferguson was just awful, and he would compound his problems by dropping his head, which the fans read as a sign that Ferguson was a poor leader. Ferguson played in only four playoff games during his time in Buffalo, and what happened in two of them served as a perfect microcosm of his career.

In the 1980 divisional-round game at San Diego, Ferguson put on a gritty display after reinjuring his sprained ankle on the first series of the game. Despite intense pain and a noticeable limp, Ferguson passed for 180 yards and nearly led the Bills to an upset over the Chargers. "I'm so proud of the way Joe played today," said coach Chuck Knox. "You saw Ferguson out there. He gave a courageous performance today. If you don't understand that, then you don't understand sports. I'm so proud of that guy just for playing."

Knox wasn't so proud the following year in the 1981 divisional round at Cincinnati. Trailing 28–21 with just under three minutes to play, Ferguson made an egregious and silly error that may have cost the Bills a spot in the AFC Championship Game.

On fourth and 3 from the Bengals 20 yard line, Ferguson threw a pass to Lou Piccone that converted the first down. However, a yellow hankie flew just as the ball was snapped, and Knox still can't believe it to this day. Ferguson had let the play clock—which was right in front of him—run out; he didn't take the snap in time. The first down was wiped out, and on fourth and 8 Ferguson overthrew an open Roland Hooks in the end zone.

In his book *By A Nose*, Bills nose tackle Fred Smerlas recalled going up to Knox's office at One Bills Drive and there was the coach watching film of the play over and over and over. "We pay that guy $600,000 a year and you mean he can't read a goddamn clock," Knox said.

Thousands of fans greet the Bills at the airport after their playoff loss at San Diego.
Buffalo Courier-Express

tage, this meant the Bills had to beat the 49ers, or they would not only fail to win the AFC East, but they also would miss the play-offs entirely.

The game was played in the rain and mud at Candlestick Park, which actually helped Ferguson's sore ankle. He played the whole game and helped the Bills pull out a breathless 18–13 victory that wasn't secure until Montana heaved two unsuccessful Hail Mary passes into the Buffalo end zone in the dying seconds.

Buffalo wasn't going to the Super Bowl, but it was going to the playoffs.

"I was thinking about it all during the week," Ferguson said of the possibility of making it back to the postseason, where he'd been for just one game in his career. "All the misery we went through for four or five years was worth it. We learned a lot going through those hardships."

With a two-week break before the AFC divisional round game in San Diego, Ferguson's ankle healed sufficiently enough for him to play, but he reinjured it early against the Chargers and was severely hobbled the rest of the day. Despite his obvious pain, Ferguson gutted it out and guided the Bills to a 14–3 halftime lead. Buffalo was still clinging to a 14–13 advantage as the game moved into its final minutes.

Right after Mike-Mayer missed a 49-yard field goal, San Diego quarterback Dan Fouts teamed with John Jefferson on a 17-yard pass to the 50 yard line. Following a pair of incompletions, Fouts dropped back on third and 10 with 2:08 left to play and hit Ron Smith over the middle on a quick post. The little-known receiver split Buffalo's defense and took it the distance for the game-winning touchdown.

It was a gut-wrenching end to such a glorious year, a loss that many players struggled to make sense of. Just as they had done the first time the Bills flew home from San Diego back in October, the fans streamed to the airport to welcome home the team, this time in defeat on a freezing cold night in January.

No, Buffalo wasn't going to the Super Bowl. But Buffalo was sure Talkin' Proud.

Jim Kelly: The Savior

Having just concluded a telephone conversation with New York State Governor Mario Cuomo, quarterback Jim Kelly looked out at the media on hand to cover the signing of his first Buffalo Bills contract in August 1986 and said, "Who knows? Maybe I'll be able to take this team to the Super Bowl and get a call from the president next."

Over the next 11 years, 11 often spectacular years and 11 years that Buffalo fans will never forget, Kelly took the Bills to four Super Bowls and forged an NFL career so prolific that his bronzed bust now resides in the Pro Football Hall of Fame. But that call from the president? Sadly, it never came.

To this day, and for all his remaining days, the greatest player in Bills history admits that the pain from losing four consecutive Super Bowls in the early 1990s will never go away, and not even his induction into the Hall of Fame in 2002 has helped to lessen the disappointment. "It never will," Kelly said. "I talked to [former Denver Broncos quarterback] John Elway and I forgot the exact words he used, but he said, 'Jim, you accomplished something that nobody will ever do again. Win or lose, that's something to be proud of.' And I said, 'Yeah, I know.' And I also know that what we accomplished will never be done again, but it would have been nice to say that we won one of them."

Kelly can't say that. Bill Parcells's New York Giants, Joe Gibbs's Washington Redskins, and Jimmy Johnson's Dallas Cowboys (twice) made sure of that by beating the Bills in Super Bowls XXV, XXVI, XXVII, and XXVIII. No doubt going 0–4 in the NFL championship game is a blight on Kelly's career, but it does not diminish what Kelly meant to the Bills and to western New York. Quite simply, as team owner Ralph Wilson has often said, "He was the most significant player in Bills' history."

Kelly was the man who almost singlehandedly saved Wilson's franchise from demise. He was the man who lifted onto his broad shoulders a dying team that was playing in a dying city and brought it back to life. A fabulous life at that. "He brought this franchise out of the gutter," said Kelly's longtime center and best friend, Kent Hull. "At the time that he came to Buffalo, they were needing a central figure to rally around. And here comes the savior. Even though we were losing that first year, he still looked good, so there was always promise. Then all of a sudden things started getting better, we started getting more people. That stuff is contagious, and it all started with the gunslinger."

The Bills owned a pair of first-round picks in the 1983 NFL draft, and there was little doubt what they were going to do with one of them. With Joe Ferguson entering his eleventh NFL season and beginning to show signs of wearing down, the Bills needed to select their quarterback of the future. And this was the year to be in need of a quarterback as players such as Kelly, Elway, Todd Blackledge, Ken O'Brien, Tony Eason, and Dan Marino were all available.

With Elway and Blackledge already gone, the Bills used the twelfth overall pick to take Notre Dame tight end Tony Hunter, filling one hole on offense. Two spots later, using a choice obtained in a trade with Cleveland, the Bills passed on Marino and grabbed Kelly, an impudent, rifle-armed kid from the University of Miami by way of East Brady, Pennsylvania.

Kay Stephenson, who had just taken the Bills head-coaching job a few months earlier when Chuck Knox left for Seattle, said, "We had an excellent draft. It would be awfully tough for me to throw cold water on this draft."

No, that would be left for Kelly. With the fledgling United States Football League competing with the NFL for the services of top-notch college players, pro football was in the midst of a tumultuous time, similar to when the American Football League burst onto the scene in the 1960s to challenge the powerfully entrenched NFL. The USFL proved to be a fly-by-night outfit, but for a couple years that league's existence gave the NFL a headache and nearly crushed the Bills franchise.

One of Kelly's agents, Greg Lustig, announced in late May 1983 that the Chicago Blitz—who owned Kelly's USFL territorial rights—were the front-runners to sign the quarterback. Lustig said the Blitz could match any monetary offer made by the Bills, and that Kelly could make much more money in endorsements playing in Chicago. Lustig said that in Chicago Kelly would enjoy "a quality of life that Buffalo cannot offer. Let's face it, the Bills can't change the fact that they're in Buffalo."

Wilson was furious, and so was someone else: Kelly's father, Joe. "I know the decision is his, but I hope it's the NFL," Joe Kelly said. "That's all he's ever talked about. And Buffalo's so close for us to drive to. I can't understand what's changed his mind. The NFL is all he's ever dreamed about."

A week later, the USFL, so desperate to bring Kelly aboard, gave Kelly's agents permission to cut a deal with any team in the league. Blitz general manager Bruce Allen agreed to this—pending proper compensation, of course—because he wanted Kelly in the league, even if he didn't play for Chicago. On June 9, Kelly made his announcement. He would play for the Houston Gamblers for more than $1 million per year, making him the USFL's second-highest paid player behind only New Jersey's Herschel Walker.

"There are risks in doing what I'm doing, but I made up my mind," Kelly said. "Everybody has to take a risk once in a while. I'm happy I did it, and I won't regret it. I always wanted to play in the NFL, but right now, the USFL is the same as the NFL. It's a business now. I did what I and my agent believed to be best for me and my career."

Obviously, this was not what was best for the Bills as the team hit rock bottom. After an 8–8 record in 1983, it all fell apart in

1984. Buffalo went 2–14 as nothing the wilting Ferguson could do at quarterback mattered, not with a defense that allowed a franchise-record 454 points. Ferguson was traded on Draft Day 1985, and that year the Bills went 2–14 again as they scored only 200 points with the laughable combination of Vince Ferragamo and Bruce Mathison at quarterback. Meanwhile, Kelly was shredding weak USFL defenses to the tune of 9,842 yards passing and 83 touchdowns in just two seasons, and when Bills fans weren't drooling, they were cursing the quarterback who spurned their team and their city. "I knew we were never going to turn things around if we didn't resolve the quarterback problem," Wilson recalled. "Everything we had seen and heard about Kelly indicated that he was the talented and brash quarterback we needed."

But heading into 1986 there was no Kelly, and no light at the end of the tunnel. The Bills were prepared to go into the season with Mathison, 1985 third-round draft pick Frank Reich, and NFL retread Art Schlichter as their quarterbacks. The only hope Bills fans had was that the USFL—known to be wobbling financially—would fold, and Kelly would have to come to Buffalo, the team that owned his playing rights.

It would be impossible to count how many novenas were recited in Buffalo, but those prayers were answered in late July when a jury in Manhattan spit in the face of a $1.7 billion antitrust suit filed by the USFL against the NFL. Needing a huge judgment in its favor to save its cash-poor operation, the USFL was put to death when the jury awarded it one dollar, trebled to three, or about enough to pay for a water bottle.

At that point the USFL failed to exist, its players were available for hire, and new Bills general manager Bill Polian sprang

Quarterback Jim Kelly and
general manager Bill Polian
Robert L. Smith Photograhy

into action. He rolled up his sleeves and dove headfirst into negotiations. After two grueling weeks—during which time Kelly tried to get the Bills to trade his rights—the historic deal was consummated. "It's funny how things turn out sometimes," Kelly says now. "I'm so happy Ralph Wilson didn't listen to me and trade me. I was doing my best to make sure it wouldn't work out between me and the Bills. I wanted them to trade me to a team like the Raiders or the Steelers. I wanted to go someplace where I would have a chance to win, and, to be honest, I didn't think the Bills were committed to winning."

You couldn't blame Kelly for his skepticism. Before his arrival, there were bumper stickers floating around western New York that read: "BRING PROFESSIONAL FOOTBALL BACK TO BUFFALO." Pro football never actually left Buffalo during the disgraceful 1984 and 1985 seasons, when the Bills were the laughingstock of the NFL, but it was hard to convince the crowds of 20,000 at Rich Stadium that the product they were watching was worthy of their hard-earned dollars.

As soon as Kelly signed that contract, the Bills gained instant respectability. They still weren't very good, but now they had a quarterback. Now they had a fighting chance.

Fred Smerlas, the Wall of Fame nose tackle who played with Kelly from 1986 through 1989, just wishes Kelly hadn't wasted two years playing in the USFL. "I thought Kelly was fabulous in college, unbelievable," said Smerlas. "When we drafted him, I thought it was going to be great, and then he went to Houston and that hurt us. But when he came to Buffalo, you knew the organization was serious now. We had some guys already in place, and we just needed a couple more players to put it together. When he came in, we knew we'd start turning it around."

The season opener that year against the Jets was a sellout, and anyone who wasn't in the stadium was watching on television as Kelly made his much-anticipated debut. Never has there been more excitement surrounding the home opener of a team that had won just four of its previous thirty-two games.

"I remember at the stadium for my first game against the Jets, there was a banner that said KELLY IS GOD, and it was like, 'Hey, that's a little too much,' " said Kelly, who threw for 292 yards and 3 touchdowns in a 28–24 loss to New York. "I guess it would have been different if the Bills had been winning, but they were coming off back-to-back 2–14 seasons. The fans needed something, and they knew if the franchise was going to stay in Buffalo, they had to start getting some players. I was one of the stepping stones."

No, he was the stepping boulder.

The reversal of fortune took time as the Bills won only two of their first nine games in 1986. But that turned out to be a positive development because, as Smerlas said, "They had to get rid of Hank before we could get anything going." Hank Bullough had taken over as head coach early in 1985 when Wilson fired Stephenson, but it was apparent that Bullough wasn't head coaching material. Smerlas called him "without a doubt, the worst head coach ever." So with the team sputtering, Wilson canned Bullough and hired Marv Levy.

Levy brought a calming, cerebral, and fatherly influence to the team, and the players responded immediately to his approach to football and life. The Bills won only two of their final seven games that year, but it was like preseason for Levy as he figured out what he had to work with, who needed to stay, and who needed to go.

The one position he knew he was solid at was quarterback. Kelly was a player you could build a franchise around, and that's what Levy, Polian, and scouting director John Butler did. "I'll say this about quarterbacks," said Hull. "They're either arrogant, cocky, or confident. Jim started out cocky, he got a little arrogant, but he wound up confident. And when you're confident, you're good, and you win."

And with Kelly at quarterback, the Bills became good—good as in six AFC East division titles, four AFC championships, and eight seasons in the playoffs while Kelly was filling the often frosty Orchard Park air with tight spirals and celebratory fist pumps.

Kelly set a team record with 285 completions his first year, and in the strike-shortened season of 1987, he earned the first of five Pro Bowl invitations while leading the Bills to a respectable 7–8 record. Then in 1988, with Kelly guiding an offense that now

Jim Kelly's Career Statistics

Year	G	Comp	Att	Pct	Yds	TD	Int
1986	16	285	480	59.4	3,593	22	17
1987	12	250	419	59.7	2,798	19	11
1988	16	269	452	59.5	3,380	15	17
1989	13	228	391	58.3	3,130	25	18
1990	14	219	346	63.3	2,829	24	9
1991	15	304	474	64.1	3,844	33	17
1992	16	269	462	58.2	3,457	23	19
1993	16	288	470	61.3	3,382	18	18
1994	14	285	448	63.6	3,114	22	17
1995	15	255	458	55.7	3,130	22	13
1996	13	222	379	58.6	2,810	14	19
Totals	160	2874	4779	60.1	35,467	237	175

included rookie running back Thurman Thomas, along with receiver Andre Reed; with Bruce Smith, Cornelius Bennett, Darryl Talley, and Smerlas anchoring a revamped defense; and with Scott Norwood making just about every kick he lined up, the Bills began their dominance of the AFC East by winning their first division title since 1980.

Their 12–4 record was highlighted by seven victories in eight games against division rivals Miami, New York, New England, and Indianapolis, plus smashing triumphs over the Raiders, Steelers, and Packers. In the first playoff game ever at Rich Stadium, Buffalo downed Warren Moon and the Houston Oilers 17–10, but a 21–10 loss at Cincinnati in the AFC Championship Game ended the season one win shy of a Super Bowl appearance.

Like many star athletes who assume leadership roles and become the face of their team, Kelly endured some uncomfortable moments in Buffalo, and a few of those came during the 1989 season when he lorded over a group that became known as the Bickering Bills.

In the second game of the year, a Monday nighter against Denver, Kelly and receiver Chris Burkett visibly argued on the sidelines. Burkett was waived soon after. When Kelly suffered a shoulder separation in the fifth game at Indianapolis, he publicly singled out tackle Howard Ballard for allowing the sack that injured him. Later in the season, Thomas took issue with Kelly for his continual sniping at teammates. When the local and national media picked up on the friction, the Bills were painted as a team divided.

"It was overblown," Kelly said. "What hurt us more than anything was the way the media handled it. Every team has bad times and good times, and if the bad times are kept in the locker room, things smooth out a lot quicker. What happened that year was it got out into the public, and the public perception started getting overblown. I take great pride in knowing that I was one of our leaders on the team. Early on I made mistakes, just like most people do, and there were things I wish I could take back that I can't. We had some problems, but they were problems that every sports team has. It's a matter of how you handle it. We were young, and I think we let the media get the best of us."

Despite the problems, the Bills won their second straight division title, but when running back Ronnie Harmon dropped a sure game-winning Kelly touchdown pass with 14 seconds left in the AFC's wild-card game at Cleveland, the season was over.

Jim Kelly's Single-Game Bests

ATTEMPTS

Date	Opponent	No.
Dec. 8, 1991	at Raiders	52
Oct. 4, 1992	vs. Dolphins	48
Nov. 7, 1993	at Patriots	46

COMPLETIONS

Date	Opponent	No.
Dec. 8, 1991	at Raiders	33
Nov. 20, 1994	vs. Packers	32
Sept. 8, 1991	vs. Steelers	31

PASSING YARDS

Date	Opponent	No.
Sept. 13, 1992	at 49ers	403
Oct. 21, 1991	vs. Bengals	392
Sept. 1, 1991	vs. Dolphins	365
Nov. 20, 1994	vs. Packers	365

And a revolution began. In the 34–30 loss to the Browns, Kelly passed for a Buffalo playoff-record and career-high 405 yards, and he did it working primarily without huddling in the second half. Offensive coordinator Ted Marchibroda thought the entire off-season about how successful Kelly was when he was in the hurry-up mode. In the 1990 opener against the Colts, the Bills ran the first series in the no-huddle offense and marched downfield to a field goal.

"We knew that our two-minute offense before the half and at the end of games was almost unstoppable," Kelly said. "I think from that point on, we realized, 'Why don't we try this all the time?' The Cleveland game was a pivotal point for us as far as running the no-huddle."

After that first series against Indianapolis, the Bills returned to a conventional offense and used the hurry-up only when it was necessary. But in a December game against Buddy Ryan's Philadelphia Eagles, the Bills unleashed the no-huddle on the NFL. Against one of the league's best defenses, Kelly threw for 229 yards and produced 24 points before the first quarter was finished.

"It was explosive," Kelly said. "Look at the people I had. Andre Reed, Don Beebe, James Lofton, Thurman behind me, and of course Kent up front. I was so excited about it. No matter what you do in your life, if you feel confident in what you're doing, everything just comes so much smoother. It was like second nature. I didn't have to do a lot of thinking, everything was just coming boom, boom, boom."

The no-huddle offense was born, and it keyed Buffalo's run to four consecutive Super Bowls, the first of which came in January 1991 when the Bills advanced to Tampa Stadium to play the New York Giants.

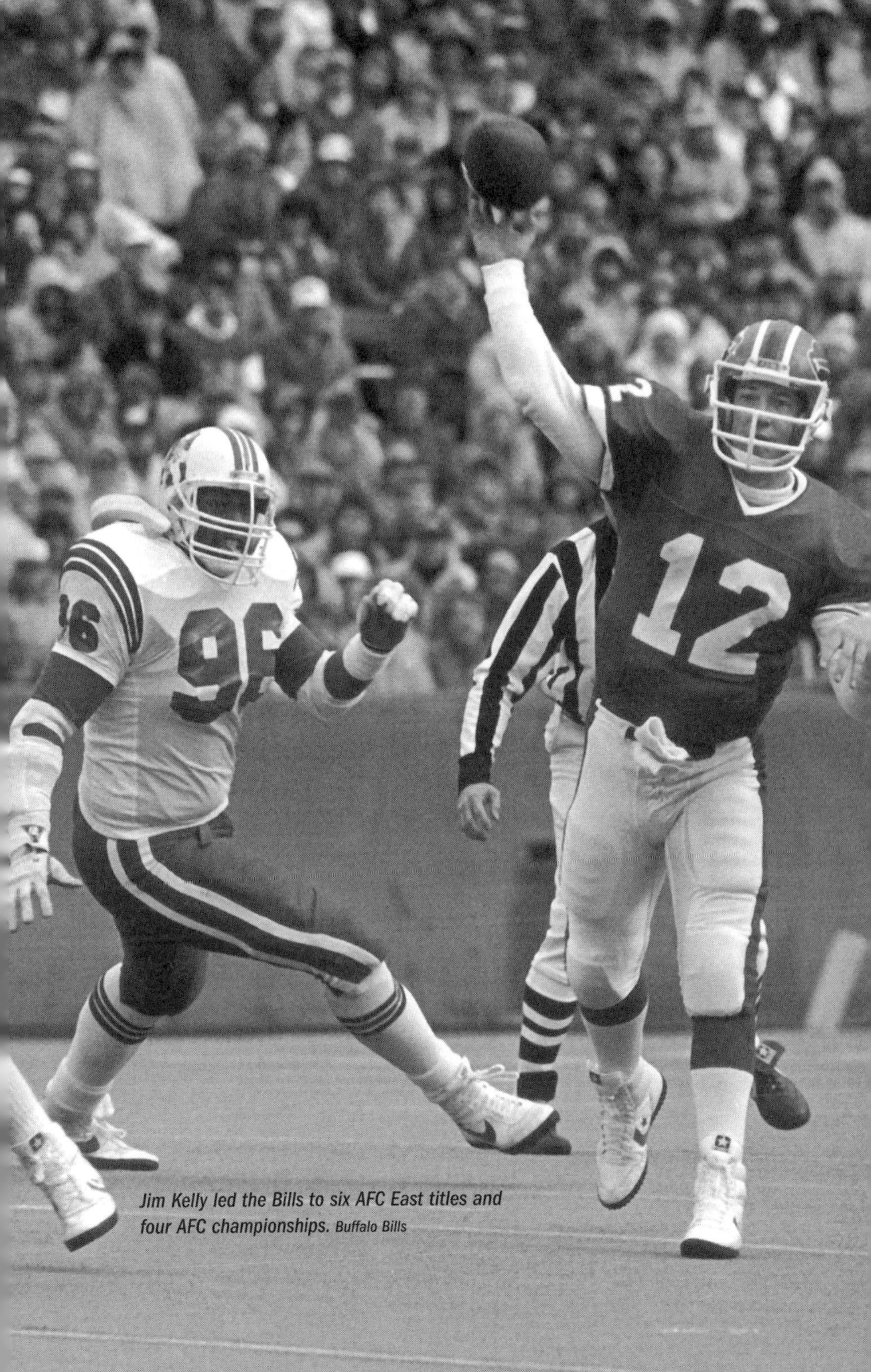

Jim Kelly led the Bills to six AFC East titles and four AFC championships. *Buffalo Bills*

Jim Kelly in the Postseason

DATE	OPPONENT	ROUND
Jan. 1, 1989	vs. Oilers	Wild-card
Jan. 8, 1989	at Bengals	AFC Champ
Jan. 6, 1990	at Browns	Division
Jan. 12, 1991	vs. Dolphins	Division
Jan. 20, 1991	vs. Raiders	AFC Champ
Jan. 27, 1991	vs. Giants	Super Bowl
Jan. 5, 1992	vs. Chiefs	Division
Jan. 12, 1992	vs. Broncos	AFC Champ
Jan. 26, 1992	vs. Redskins	Super Bowl
Jan. 17, 1993	vs. Dolphins	AFC Champ
Jan. 31, 1993	vs. Cowboys	Super Bowl
Jan. 15, 1994	vs. Raiders	Division
Jan. 23, 1994	vs. Chiefs	AFC Champ
Jan. 30, 1994	vs. Cowboys	Super Bowl
Dec. 30, 1995	vs. Dolphins	Wild-card
Jan. 6, 1996	at Steelers	Division
Dec. 28, 1996	vs. Jaguars	Wild-card

Totals: **17 Games**

RESULT	COMP	ATT	YD	TD	INT
W, 17–10	19	33	244	0	1
L, 21–10	14	30	163	1	3
L, 34–30	28	54	405	3	2
W, 44–34	19	29	339	3	1
W, 51–3	17	23	300	2	1
L, 20–19	18	30	212	0	0
W, 37–14	23	35	273	3	3
W, 10–7	13	25	117	0	2
L, 37–24	28	58	275	2	4
W, 29–10	17	24	177	1	2
L, 52–17	4	7	82	0	2
W, 29–23	27	37	287	2	0
W, 30–13	17	27	160	0	0
L, 30–13	31	50	260	0	1
W, 37–22	12	22	195	1	2
L, 40–21	14	29	135	1	3
L, 30–27	21	32	239	1	1
(9–8)	322	545	3,863	20	28

Of the four title games Kelly played in, Super Bowl XXV was by far his best performance, but it wasn't good enough. In the game's dying moments, Kelly drove the Bills to the Giants 29 yard line, setting up a 47-yard field-goal attempt for Norwood. It was no better than a fifty-fifty proposition that Norwood would make the kick, and, unfortunately for the Bills, the kick drifted wide right. "I don't think anyone in Buffalo will ever forget that," Kelly said of the vision of the ball failing to split the goalposts. "It was a heartbreak because we were the best team in the NFL that year, and we were the best team that day."

Buffalo would play in the next three Super Bowls but never came even remotely close to winning. With Kelly missing the final two games of 1994, the Bills failed to make the playoffs for the first time since 1987, but they rebounded in 1995 to win another division crown. They then defeated Miami in the wild-card round at Rich Stadium, sending long-time Dolphins coach Don Shula into retirement on a downer.

The following week, Kelly returned home to western Pennsylvania to play the Steelers at Three Rivers Stadium, and Pittsburgh gave him a rude welcome. He was knocked out of the game briefly in the third quarter and wound up throwing 3 interceptions as the Steelers rolled to a 40–21 victory.

Kelly's final year in 1996 proved just as disappointing. The Bills made the playoffs as a wild-card team, but they suffered their first postseason loss ever at Rich Stadium, falling to the two-year-old upstart Jacksonville Jaguars. Kelly's career ended with him being carted off the field to a standing ovation after getting his bell rung late in the game. On the play he lost a fumble that the Jaguars converted into a game-winning field goal by Mike Hollis with 3:07 left to play.

As the fans filed out of the stadium that day, there was a sense that an era had come to an end. Rumors had been circulating throughout the year that Kelly—whose contract was up at the end of the season—would not be returning. Sure enough, a month later, at a packed press conference that was televised live by local stations as well as ESPN, Kelly announced his retirement. It was a day filled with tears, but a day also filled with remembrances of a career so richly satisfying.

Today, Kelly continues to live in Orchard Park. He spends much of his time raising money and awareness for Hunter's Hope, the foundation he started in the name of his son, Hunter, who was born with the insidious Krabbe's Disease.

As he looks back on his life in football, particularly the eleven glorious years he played in Buffalo, Kelly makes sure it is plainly clear that while he may have been the star performer, his supporting cast was second to none, and that he wouldn't have achieved what he did without such a fabulous team. "I always knew, and I was always brought up believing, that you can't do things alone. I know I was a key ingredient because of the position I played; I knew that in order for the Bills to go anywhere they had to have a top quarterback. I was able to get people to not so much follow me, but to join me, and I had enough people join me."

The Architects of Success

The Bills would not have gone to four consecutive Super Bowls in the early 1990s without the on-field performances of star players such as Jim Kelly, Thurman Thomas, Bruce Smith, Andre Reed, Kent Hull, Darryl Talley, and Steve Tasker. Likewise, the Bills would not have been the Bills without the off-field performances of general manager Bill Polian, coach Marv Levy, and director of personnel John

Butler—the magnificent front-office triumvirate that rebuilt the team literally from the ground up from the middle to late 1980s.

"You had a guy who could coach 'em, a guy who could find 'em, and a guy who could sign 'em," said Hull. "It was Marv telling John what he wanted, and John going out and finding these guys, and Bill going out and signing them. That was a hell of a team."

And together they built one hell of a team.

Polian, the fiery red-headed Irishman, arrived in western New York first, joining the Bills in 1984. The Bronx native graduated from New York University in 1965 and began his career in football shortly thereafter, working ten years combined as an assistant at Manhattan College, the U.S. Merchant Marine Academy, and at Columbia University. He was given his first chance in pro football in 1976 when Levy—then coach and general manager of the Canadian Football League's Montreal Alouettes—hired him to be a scout.

Levy had asked his assistant, Bob Windisch, to line up some part-timers to scout NFL training camps. Polian was on the list, and when Levy saw Polian's work, he had to hire him. "I didn't know Bill from Adam," Levy recalled. "But after reading his reports, I wanted to get to know him. I remember saying to Bob, 'This stuff is so thorough, so meticulous, we need to hire the man who compiled these.' " And so began a relationship that through the years thrived professionally and personally to the point where Levy asked Polian to present him when Levy was inducted into the Pro Football Hall of Fame in 2001.

When Levy was hired by Lamar Hunt to be the Kansas City Chiefs head coach in 1978, he brought Polian with him to the NFL as a pro scout. When Levy was fired five years later following the 1982 season, Polian was swept out the door with him, though Polian landed on his feet back in Canada as player personnel director for the Winnipeg Blue Bombers.

Winnipeg would go on to win the Grey Cup (Canada's equivalent of the Super Bowl) in 1984, but Polian was not there to enjoy the fruits of his labor. At the conclusion of the 1983 season, he couldn't resist reuniting with Levy when Levy was hired to be the head coach of the Chicago Blitz of the United States Football League. Polian spent the spring of 1984 as the team's pro personnel director, and once the USFL season ended, he was on the move again. This time it was back to the NFL, where Ralph Wilson hired him in Buffalo to be his director of pro personnel in August of 1984. This is when Polian began to build his legacy.

After the Bills sank to the depths of the NFL with a 2–14 record, Terry Bledsoe the team GM, suffered a heart attack in February 1985. Though it was announced that Polian, scouting director Norm Pollom, and his assistant, Bruce Nicholas, would share Bledsoe's duties, Polian took the lead and ran with it.

The Bills owned the number-one pick in the 1985 draft, and they targeted Virginia Tech defensive end Bruce Smith. Polian began negotiations with Smith's agent well before the draft, and by selection day it was a done deal. Smith became the cornerstone of the massive rebuilding project, and Andre Reed, an unknown wide receiver out of tiny Kutztown (Pennsylvania) State, whom Polian plucked in the fourth round, would prove to be the second block laid in place.

Another 2–14 nightmare ensued in 1985, and when the season mercifully came to an end, Bledsoe was fired two days before Christmas. Polian was named as his replacement. "Really,

I didn't know Bill all that well," said Wilson. "I just appointed him GM to see how well he'd do. I didn't call around the league asking, 'What do you know about Bill Polian?' I know that doesn't sound too smart, but that's what I did."

It was one of the smartest decisions Wilson ever made. And then Polian made one of the smartest decisions he ever made.

After Polian signed Jim Kelly to be the Bills quarterback in August 1986, expectations began to rise in Buffalo. But when the team continued to struggle under coach Hank Bullough, Polian knew a change was in order. "We were 2–7, and it was obvious that the players just weren't responding to Hank; he had lost the team," Polian recalled. "I went to Ralph Wilson and said, 'Mr. Wilson, there's only one man I'd recommend to turn this around, and that man's name is Marv Levy.' I told him how Marv had rebuilt the program in Kansas City, but that the NFL players strike [in 1982] came along and everything fell apart. Mr. Wilson called Lamar Hunt, and Mr. Hunt told him that he had made a mistake firing Marv. That was good enough for Mr. Wilson. The rest, as they say, is history."

Of course there was much consternation and hand-wringing in Buffalo over Wilson's and Polian's choice. Levy was a gray-haired, sixty-one-year-old with a 31–42 career NFL record, all at Kansas City. This was the man who was going to turn around the fortunes of a sagging team? Levy may have been Harvard educated, but Bills fans weren't looking for a scholar, they were looking for a Lombardi.

"There was a lot of skepticism on the part of the fans and the media, and I understood that because I had made some coaching decisions in the past that you might say didn't exactly work out," said Wilson. "But I had a strong feeling things would be different

Marv Levy coached
the Bills to four AFC
championships.
Buffalo Bills

under Marv. He was a very, very impressive person, extremely intelligent. He had a great knowledge of the game of football and a great sense of humor. I just had this intuition that he would be the perfect person to turn things around. I really believed he would hit a home run for us."

Or four, as in four consecutive AFC championships from 1990 to 1993.

"I remember Marv said if you give a coach four years, he'll eliminate things that he inherited, he'll replace it with his personality, and he'll make a winner out of a team," said Hull. It was one of many things Levy told his players during his unmatched tenure in Buffalo, when he posted a record of 123–78 (counting the playoffs) and not only taught his adoring players lessons about football, but also about life. Some players didn't always get his references and analogies, many having to do with World War II, but they always knew that whatever Levy was espousing, it was pertinent, and they'd get it eventually.

Levy knew that, which is part of his charm. One time he alluded to the German army's overconfidence during World War II and the importance of crossing one river at a time, like Hannibal. "To be honest," Levy said, "I don't know how many of these guys even know what World War II was, and they probably think Hannibal is an offensive tackle for the Jets."

Kelly laughs now when he recalls some of Levy's motivational speeches, but he wasn't laughing then because he revered Levy and was mesmerized by his knowledge and his manner. "I've always respected everything Marv said," Kelly said. "I know my career wouldn't have gone the same way if he wasn't my head coach. Not only from the standpoint of being a coach who allowed me to take control of a team and take control of an

The Professor Speaks

Schooled in literature at Harvard, Marv Levy may have been the NFL's most studious coach. His pregame speeches became legendary in the Buffalo locker room because he constantly used words that many of his players had never heard. When asked if he would be attending Levy's Hall of Fame induction in 2001, linebacker Darryl Talley said, "I want to be there just to see what new words I can learn by listening to Marv's speech."

Kent Hull, the Pro Bowl center in the middle of Buffalo's no-huddle offense during the Super Bowl years, once said, "My vocabulary improved tenfold playing for Marv. There was a whole lot of head-shaking going on when Marv used those $10 words you've never heard of. Heck, for all I knew, he could have been making those words up."

Levy was a master at coming up with neat little catch phrases to emphasize his points. Here are just a few:

- "World War II was a must win."

- "What you do should speak so loudly that no one can hear what you say."

- "Everyone wants to win. The special person has the will to prepare to win."

- "Adversity is an opportunity for heroism."

- "Expect rejection, but expect more to overcome it."

- "If Michelangelo wanted to play it safe, he would have painted the floor of the Sistine Chapel."

- "Where would you rather be than right here, right now?"

- "The coach that starts listening to the fans winds up sitting next to them."

offense, but also being the person that I am because I learned so much from him. I took so much out of everything he said. People would laugh when he'd talk about Churchill or Patton or whoever. I always fed off his speeches, and I always took everything to heart. I think most people on our team did. That's why we made it to five AFC Championship Games and made it to four straight Super Bowls. I owe most of my career to Marv Levy."

Levy was the son of Jewish immigrants who came to the United States from England at the turn of the twentieth century, settling in Chicago. His father ran a produce market and was an accomplished basketball player. He would later serve heroically in World War I. His intelligent mother took care of the house and taught her son to love literature and history.

Expertly using both sides of the gene pool, Levy became an accomplished athlete and student. He attended Coe College in Iowa, where he starred in football and track and earned a Phi Beta Kappa key that he used to gain admission to Harvard Law School.

After a month at Harvard, Levy realized he had no desire to become an attorney. His heart was in teaching and coaching. He transferred to Harvard's graduate school, where he earned a degree in English history, but once he left school, the pull of coaching was irresistible. He telephoned his father to break the news to him and, after a long pause, Sam Levy told his son, "Be a good one."

Levy's first job was at St. Louis Country Day School in Missouri in 1951, beginning a coaching odyssey that lasted forty-seven years. He stopped along the way at college campuses such as Coe, the University of New Mexico, California, and William and Mary, before finally landing his first job in the NFL as an assistant with the Philadelphia Eagles in 1969. A year later, George Allen hired him to be the special teams coach of the Los Angeles Rams, and he followed Allen to Washington, where he helped the Redskins reach Super Bowl VII in January 1973.

After the Redskins lost the Super Bowl to Miami—something Levy unfortunately would come to perfect during his time in Buffalo—Levy migrated north of the border to become head coach in Montreal, leading the Alouettes to two Grey Cup titles in five years. That success piqued NFL interest, and Kansas City hired him in 1978. Levy's Chiefs improved each of his first four years, from 4–12 to 7–9 to 8–8 to 9–7, but the NFL players strike shredded the team in 1982. It finished 3–6, and Levy was replaced by John Mackovic.

Being hired by the Bills was almost like a mulligan of sorts for Levy. He didn't think anyone in the NFL would be interested in him thanks to his uninspiring record with the Chiefs, plus the fact that he was six decades old and had been out of the league for four years. But Wilson took a chance, and Levy was thrilled to come to Buffalo. He saw the Bills as a team that had tremendous upside despite its recent woes.

"I was licking my chops because I saw Buffalo as a sleeping giant," Levy said. "First of all, I walked into a great meeting room with guys like Jim Kelly, Andre Reed, Bruce Smith, young guys who hadn't quite yet blossomed. They had been a poor team prior, so they had some pretty good draft choices, and they had a lot of them stockpiled and ready to go. And I knew I was coming to work for a fantastic general manager because I'd known Bill from before and known all his qualities, so I was encouraged about that. I thought if we avoided catastrophic injuries, I believed we could turn it around in a hurry."

Bill Polian (left) recommended
Marv Levy for the Bills head
coaching job.
Buffalo Bills

Levy used the final seven games of 1986, during which the Bills went 2–5, to determine who to weed out and what areas of the team needed upgrading. Levy formulated a workable plan, but before he and Polian could get around to fixing the engine, they needed to add one more spark plug. "We needed to hire a director of player personnel, and we interviewed a ton of people, many of them high profile," Levy said. "One of them was a scout who had worked with us for the Chicago Blitz, John Butler, whom we liked. We did it as a courtesy. When he walked out, Bill and I looked at each other and said, 'He's the guy.' He blew us away."

Like Levy, Butler was born in Chicago. After he graduated from Urbana (Illinois) High School, he served in the Marine Corps for four years. That stint included a fourteen-month tour of combat duty in Vietnam, where he rose to the rank of sergeant. After being released from the military, he enrolled at San Bernardino Junior College and played football for two seasons before transferring back home to play for the University of Illinois. However, his career was cut short after one season with the Fighting Illini by a knee injury.

Even though he couldn't play, Butler knew his future was in football. He spent six years coaching at the high school level and another three as a part-time assistant at the University of Evansville (Indiana). He was making $3,500 a year and working nights at a 7-Eleven during this time. Only his passion for football kept him going. He finally was given his big break by the same man who had given Levy his first break in pro football: George Allen.

Allen was general manager and head coach of the Chicago Blitz in 1983, and he hired Butler to be a college scout. Butler knew immediately that scouting, not coaching, was his forte, and he thrived in the position.

After the 1983 USFL season, the owners of the Chicago and Arizona franchises decided to swap teams. Butler was not part of the Chicago package headed to Arizona, but when Polian became the new personnel man in Chicago, Allen recommended to Polian that he retain Butler on his scouting staff. Butler stayed with the Blitz, rising to the position of director of college scouting until the team folded its operation in 1985. His reputation had already generated interest, and he wound up signing as a scout for the NFL's San Diego Chargers. Two years later, he took up residence in Orchard Park and, along with Levy and Polian, began the process of building the AFC's best team four years running.

With Levy grabbing headlines as the head coach and Polian winning NFL executive of the year awards, Butler's role in the remaking of the Bills is often overlooked, but it shouldn't be. His first draft in 1987 netted players such as Shane Conlan, Nate Odomes, Jamie Mueller, Leon Seals, Keith McKeller, and Howard Ballard, all future starters. In 1988 the Bills didn't have a first-round pick, and he was positive that running back Thurman Thomas would be a steal in the second round if the Bills could get him. The Bills did, along with late-round finds John Hagy, Jeff Wright, and Carlton Bailey.

In 1989 Butler unearthed speedy wide receiver Don Beebe from Chadron (Nebraska) State, and in 1990 the final pieces of the first Super Bowl team were gathered in the draft as J. D. Williams, Carwell Gardner, Glenn Parker, Marvcus Patton, Mike Lodish, and Al Edwards were selected.

"John Butler was probably one of the most outstanding personnel people in the league," said Hull. "If you needed somebody, he could find him. And it wouldn't always be from Ohio

John Butler played a key role in building the Bills into champions. Buffalo Bills

State or USC, it might be someone from Chadron or Kutztown or Alabama State. He knew how to find these people, and he found people who fit Marv's philosophy."

Which is why the trio of Polian-Levy-Butler was so wildly successful during its six seasons together. Collectively, those men led the Bills to four AFC East division titles and three AFC championships. After Polian was let go following the 1992 season, Butler was promoted to general manager, and he and Levy produced another two divisions titles and one AFC championship.

Polian spent one year working in the league office, then governed the birth of the expansion Carolina Panthers as their first general manager and saw that team reach the NFC Championship Game in just its second season of existence in 1996.

Prior to the 1998 season, he became president of the Indianapolis Colts, and he remains there today.

Levy retired following the 1997 season and stayed close to the NFL by moving smoothly into the broadcast booth. Since his induction into the Hall of Fame, he has cut back his schedule and is finally enjoying the life of a retired man.

Butler lasted in Buffalo until the final week of the 2000 season, when Wilson fired him. Butler then took over the operation in San Diego and was the Chargers general manager and executive vice president until cancer took his life at age fifty-six in the spring of 2003.

"I don't think any of us ever talked turf; nobody ever said, 'That's my call,' " said Levy of his time in Buffalo working with his two good friends. "There was no, 'You better be right.' If John said we ought to draft this guy, and it didn't work out, okay, we moved on. It just worked out. You talk about good luck. The relationship I had with those guys. We just had a totally trusting working relationship."

WELCOME TO
TIME OUTS
DOWN
TO GO

The Winningest Losers of Them All

In the week leading up to the 2003 NFC Championship Game between the Philadelphia Eagles and the Carolina Panthers, a member of the Eagles was quoted as saying he didn't want his team to be remembered as the next Buffalo Bills. "I thought, 'Well, buddy, you don't have to worry about that,' " said Darryl Talley, the former linebacker and spiritual leader of the Bills. "The Eagles weren't even the best in their conference. We were the best in ours four years in a row. How many teams can make that claim now? How many ever will?"

Perhaps none.

The Eagles of 2003 had lost back-to-back NFC Championship Games when that comment was made, and then they lost their third in a row, 14–3, to the Panthers. No, they won't be remembered as the modern-day Bills. They couldn't hold a candle to the Bills of the early 1990s, the Bills who won four straight AFC championships, a remarkable achievement that goes wholly unnoticed because Buffalo proceeded to lose four straight Super Bowls, another feat that probably never will be duplicated.

Back then, when the Bills were losing year after year in the ultimate game, they became a national joke, the loveable losers, the "serial killers of the Super Bowl" as *New York Daily News* columnist Mike Lupica famously dubbed them. But as time passes and the magnitude of what Buffalo accomplished hits you like a Bruce Smith sack or a Kent Hull block, football followers have come to appreciate the Bills.

Losers?

In the sense that they never won the big one, yes, the Bills were the losers in four NFL championship games. But no team that between 1990 and 1993 went 49–15 in regular-season games, also winning nine straight AFC playoff games and earning thirty-six Pro Bowl invitations can be considered losers. "The only thing we can be accused of is not finishing those great seasons," said Talley. Added quarterback Jim Kelly: "Had we won just one of those games, they'd be talking about us as one of the greatest teams of all time."

This is how the Bills won four consecutive AFC championships—and lost four consecutive Super Bowls.

1990

It was a rare moment in the coaching career of Marv Levy when he showed genuine displeasure with the way his team played. Levy was a regular on NFL Films, yelling at officials and calling them "over officious jerks," but he never derided his team in public. However, in the wake of a laughable 35–7 loss to the Chicago Bears in South Carolina, which closed a winless preseason for the Bills, Levy said, "I'm sick and humiliated about how our team played. I apologize to the people here in South Carolina, to Buffalo Bills fans, and it damn well isn't going to happen again."

Over the next four years, it rarely did.

The Bills heard their coach loud and clear and opened the season with a rollicking 26–10 victory over Indianapolis, unveiling the no-huddle offense on the first series of the game. Quarterback Jim Kelly, recalling the exhausted looks on the faces of the offensive line when they went to the sideline after that possession, said, "When we came off the field, the offensive line said, 'We're not going to do that again, are we?' "

The Bills didn't do it again until December, when they nearly ran coach Buddy Ryan's Eagles out of Rich Stadium with a 24-point first quarter en route to a 30–23 victory. In between the Bills were routed in Miami in week 2, then reeled off eight straight victories before a Monday night loss to Houston, prompting ABC announcer Al Michaels to predict "the road to the Super Bowl will probably go through Buffalo."

Michaels' prognostication proved correct, but not before the Bills negotiated a treacherous detour. During a 17–13 victory over the New York Giants at the Meadowlands in what turned out to be a Super Bowl preview, Kelly suffered a knee injury that would knock him out for a month. Yet even without their star quarterback, the Bills went home the next week and whipped Miami 24–14 to win the AFC East title, as Frank Reich passed for 234 yards and 2 touchdowns, and Thurman Thomas rushed for 154 yards and another score.

Buffalo's 13–3 record gave it homefield advantage for the playoffs, and the bye week gave the recuperating Kelly just enough time to get ready. He returned to lead the Bills to a pulsating 44–34 victory over the Dolphins in the divisional round, putting on a dazzling no-huddle show by throwing for 339 yards and 3 touchdowns on a snow-slicked field.

A day later, even though Bo Jackson suffered a hip injury that ultimately ended his NFL career, the Raiders downed Cincinnati 20–10 to earn a trip to Buffalo for the AFC Championship Game. And then two days after that, the United States and its allies went to war with Iraq, as hundreds of planes unleashed a massive attack on targets there and in occupied Kuwait. The start of the Persian Gulf War immediately cast doubt on whether the NFL would play its upcoming conference championship games, but commissioner Paul Tagliabue said, "We're going to monitor the events in the Middle East right up until kickoff Sunday. And if the networks believe the events in the gulf are so dramatic or so significant that they should go to an all-news format, then we would not play our games."

On game day emotions were at an all-time high at Rich Stadium. The Bills were hosting their first championship game since 1964, but with the lives of American troops in danger half a world away, there was a noticeable tension in the air. "We have to realize what we're doing here is not that big a deal," said Bills tight end Pete Metzelaars. "It is to some people, but we're not

*Thurman Thomas gave the Bills a
nearly unstoppable ground attack.*
Buffalo Bills

talking about losing our lives. We're just out there playing a game."

To their credit it was the game of their lives. The Bills humiliated the proud Raiders 51–3, thanks to a 41-point avalanche in the first half. Kelly passed for 300 yards, the Bills amassed 502 yards on offense, and the defense intercepted 6 Raiders passes. "If they play like they did today, there's nobody who's going to beat them, plain and simple," said Raiders defensive end Howie Long.

But the Bills didn't play the same way against the Giants in Super Bowl XXV at Tampa Stadium. Bill Parcells's team combated the lethal no-huddle offense with a ball-control attack and held possession for more than forty minutes, effectively keeping Machine Gun Kelly on the sidelines. Meanwhile, when Kelly was on the field, he was confronted with a confusing two-man defensive line formation conceived by defensive coordinator Bill Belichick that officially stamped Belichick (now the New England Patriots head coach) as a master innovator.

The teams traded first-quarter field goals before the Bills embarked on an 80-yard drive that ended with Don Smith scoring on a 1-yard plunge early in the second quarter. A few minutes later, Buffalo punter Rick Tuten pinned the Giants back at their 7 yard line, setting the stage for Bruce Smith's sack of New York quarterback Jeff Hostetler for a safety and a 12–3 Bills advantage.

The Bills seemed to be in control of the game, but the defense let down on back-to-back New York possessions that bridged the second and third quarters. Hostetler—playing because starter Phil Simms had been knocked out for the season by the Bills back in the December game—drove the Giants 87 yards in the final four minutes of the half, hitting Stephen Baker with a 14-yard touchdown pass. After the lengthy halftime break, the Giants consumed the first 9:29 of the third quarter with a 14-play, 75-yard odyssey that ended with Ottis Anderson's touchdown plunge that gave New York a 17–12 lead.

Buffalo regained the lead when Thomas broke a 31-yard touchdown run on the first play of the fourth quarter, but another interminable New York drive took 7:32 off the clock and resulted in Matt Bahr's go-ahead, 21-yard field goal to make the score 20–19 Giants with 7:20 remaining.

After an exchange of punts, Buffalo took possession at its own 10 yard line with 2:16 to play, and Kelly trotted onto the field looking to direct a game-winning drive. "This is what champions are made of," Kelly said in the huddle. "Let's be one."

They came so close. Thomas's 22-yard run converted a third and 1 and moved the ball to Buffalo's 41, and a Kelly scramble gained a first down at the Giants 46, but forced him to spend his final timeout with 48 seconds to go. A 6-yard pass to Keith McKeller, an 11-yard run by Thomas, and a deliberate clock-killing spike by Kelly left the ball at the Giants 29 with 8 seconds to play. On came kicker Scott Norwood to attempt the first win-or-else field goal in Super Bowl history.

Wide right.

Arguably the most despicable phrase in the Buffalo lexicon, right up there with "lake-effect snow." It was the ultimate heartbreak for the Bills and their fans, watching Norwood's 47-yard attempt sail outside the right upright. This would be the closest the Bills would come to winning a Super Bowl, but there were still three maddening, painful Super Bowl defeats to follow.

Forever Wide Right

The day after Scott Norwood missed what remains today the only win-or-lose field goal attempt in Super Bowl history, he wasn't sure what to expect when he returned to Buffalo with the team for a welcome home party in Niagara Square. Those tears that filled his eyes were not because the overflow crowd estimated at more than 30,000 people booed him off the makeshift stage. Instead, he cried because the fans cheered him wildly, providing a loving embrace that he so desperately needed.

"I know I've never felt more loved than I do right now," Norwood told the crowd when it was his turn to speak.

Norwood's 47-yard, wide-right kick in Super Bowl XXV is the only one of its kind because had he made it, Buffalo would have won the game; because he missed it, the New York Giants were 20–19 victors. Baltimore's Jim O'Brien (Super Bowl V) and New England's Adam Vinatieri (Super Bowl XXXVI and XXXVIII) made their winning kicks when the score was tied, so if they had missed, overtime would have ensued.

Norwood kicked one more year for the Bills, and he made a field goal in Super Bowl XXVI. But he was released prior to 1992, and his NFL career ended quietly. He has never been able to escape the fact that he missed the kick at Tampa Stadium, but he has moved on with his life and is living happily in Virginia with his wife and three children, working as a financial planner.

"A lot of people thought my life was ruined, but nothing could be further from the truth," he said. "I'm very happy and contented. I have a loving wife, three children who keep me very busy, and a lot of fond football memories. Sure I wish I had made that kick, but my life didn't go into a tailspin. I wasn't so much hurting because of the kick itself. The kick was about the people. It wasn't about anything else. It wasn't about monetary gain or some great stature for myself or anything else. When you talk about the Buffalo Bills, it really is about the community and the people who support it. They had a lot of emotions invested in us. It was an emotional time. I just felt bad for the people."

1991

With the no-huddle officially entrenched as their mode of operation, the Bills ran through their regular-season schedule, once again winning 13 of 16 games to capture their fourth straight AFC East crown.

Buffalo set team records for most points (458), touchdowns (58), first downs (359), net yards (6,252), and passing yards (3,871, since broken), as Kelly enjoyed his greatest statistical season with 3,844 yards passing, 33 touchdowns, and a quarterback rating of 97.6. "You go through training camp and you see how things are clicking and you know things are going to start working," Kelly recalled of that 1991 season. "We were still catching people off guard, it wasn't like it was three years into it and people were starting to catch on to what we were doing."

The Bills beat Miami 35–31 in the opener thanks to a team-record 582 yards, and then Kelly threw a career-best 6 scoring passes in a 52–34 blowout of Pittsburgh. Former San Francisco coach Bill Walsh, the father of the West Coast offense who was now a television analyst, was wowed by the no-huddle and ranked it "in the spectacular category. Are we talking about the greatest offense ever? I don't know, we have to wait and see what happens over sixteen games. But yes, no question, I'm very impressed."

The Bills won their first five games and ten of their first eleven, and by Thanksgiving the AFC East and homefield advantage were virtually decided.

On the way to Minneapolis for Super Bowl XXVI, the Bills earned two polar opposite playoff victories. In the divisional round, the no-huddle was on fire in a 37–14 rout of Kansas City, as Kelly passed for 273 yards and Thomas rushed for 100. But in the AFC Championship Game against John Elway's Denver Broncos, defense ruled the day. The game was scoreless until the fortieth minute, when nose tackle Jeff Wright batted an Elway pass into the air, and the ball fell softly into linebacker Carlton Bailey's arms. Bailey then rumbled 11 yards to the end zone for a touchdown to key a nail-biting, 10–7 victory.

Buffalo's second Super Bowl opponent was Washington, easy 41–10 victors in the NFC Championship Game over Detroit, and while the Redskins spent Super Bowl week making headway on their game plan, the Bills spent the week making headlines. First, Bruce Smith used the Super Bowl stage to announce that he had been receiving hate mail with racist overtones from Buffalo fans angry that he had missed most of the season due to a knee injury. Then Thurman Thomas, apparently upset that offensive coordinator Ted Marchibroda called Kelly "the Michael Jordan of the offense" skipped a mandatory press conference. Thomas appeared the next day, apologized, and said he thought he was "the Michael Jordan of the offense."

To say the least, it was not an ideal week for the Bills, and things only got worse on game day. Thomas misplaced his helmet and missed the first two plays of the game, and when he finally made it onto the field, it mattered little. The Redskins defense held him to 13 yards on 10 attempts, intercepted 4 Kelly passes, and raced to a 37–10 lead before settling for a 37–24 victory.

After a scoreless first quarter, the game got out of hand quickly as Washington scored 17 points in the first eight minutes of the second quarter. The Bills finally mounted a threat late in the half, but an obvious pass interference call on Washington deep in Redskins territory against Andre Reed went uncalled, and when Reed slammed his helmet in disgust and drew an unsportsmanlike penalty, the Bills were pushed out of field-goal range. Any hopes of a second-half comeback were shattered on the first play of the third quarter, when linebacker Kurt Gouveia picked off Kelly's pass and returned it to the Bills 2 yard line to set up Gerald Riggs's touchdown plunge.

"You only get so many chances," said Kelly. "I'll be thirty-two next month. Time's running out on me. This is hard to take because we have such a good team. We've come a long way. You hate to say, 'There's always next year.' "

Sadly, Kelly would say that two more times.

1992

The Bills took a different approach to their third straight Super Bowl appearance. After a blazing 4–0 start that saw them score no fewer than 34 points in any game, the ship began to spring some leaks.

One-sided losses to the Dolphins and Raiders slowed down the charge, and, after an impressive five-game winning streak left the Bills with a 9–2 record and a one-game lead over Miami in the AFC East, the team slumped in the final month as Miami stole the division crown. The Bills season-ending, 27–3 blowout loss at Houston dropped the team to wild-card status, and, worse, Kelly suffered a knee injury against the Oilers that would force him to miss the first two playoff games.

Of course two minutes into the third quarter of the wild-card game against Houston, it looked as if there wouldn't be a second game to worry about. The Oilers were ahead 35–3 in front of a silent gathering at Rich Stadium. And then Kenneth Davis scored on a short run, and the ever-reliable backup Reich threw 4 touchdown passes, including 3 straight to Reed. After the Oilers somehow regrouped to force overtime, Steve Christie capped the greatest comeback in NFL history with a 32-yard field goal for a miraculous 41–38 victory. Rather than packing up and going home, the Bills were packing up and heading to Pittsburgh for a divisional-round game.

Kelly still couldn't play, but the Bills didn't need him. Reich threw a pair of touchdown passes and the defense forced three Steelers turnovers during an easy 24–3 victory at Three Rivers Stadium.

Now it was on to Miami to play the hated Dolphins for the AFC championship at Joe Robbie Stadium. In the week leading up to the game, Kelly's status was the hot topic. Many followers of the team felt Levy should stick with the red-hot Reich. But Kelly was Buffalo's quarterback—there was no doubt about that in Levy's mind—and when he was given medical clearance to play, he was the choice.

Again, it really didn't matter. Buffalo's defense was superb, forcing 5 Dolphins turnovers and holding them to 33 rushing yards, and Christie kicked 5 field goals during a 29–10 laugher. The Bills thus equaled Miami's feat in the mid-70s of three straight Super Bowl berths.

The difference between those Dolphins and these Bills is that Miami split its first two Super Bowls and won the third. Buffalo lost the first two, then became the first team in history to lose three in a row. And the Bills didn't just lose Super Bowl XXVII, they embarrassed themselves as the Dallas Cowboys took advantage of 9 Buffalo turnovers to win in a rout, 52–17.

It began so well when Steve Tasker blocked a Dallas punt at the Cowboys 16 yard line, and the Bills scored four plays later on Thomas's 2-yard run. But then the Bills decided to star in their own version of the football follies. A Kelly interception led to a

The Bills tough-as-nails defense was anchored by Bruce Smith.

Buffalo Bills

Troy Aikman touchdown pass, and a penalty on the ensuing kickoff forced Buffalo to start the next drive at its own 10 yard line. The undeniable unraveling occurred on the next play. Kelly was sacked by Charles Haley and lost the ball, not to mention the use of his left knee. Jimmy Jones scooped up the ball and fell into the end zone to put the Cowboys ahead for good, while the Buffalo training staff scooped up Kelly and brought him to the sidelines, where he spent the rest of the long, miserable day.

Reich helped pull the Bills within 14–10, but Aikman threw 2 touchdown passes to Michael Irvin in an 18-second span in the final two minutes of the second quarter—the latter set up by a Thomas fumble—and the second half became irrelevant.

"We've got the talent, but if you don't make the plays, it doesn't mean a damn thing," said Smith. "We knew we were going to make history tonight one way or the other, but we didn't want to make it this way." Said Darryl Talley: "We're a good enough team to get here three consecutive times and to not win once, it's a crying shame."

And still, there was one more to go.

1993

By now the Bills had become the butt of countless jokes, but they remained undeterred in their quest for Super Bowl glory. Bill Polian was replaced as general manager by John Butler; the Bills lost left tackle Will Wolford and linebacker Shane Conlan in free agency, said good-bye to aging wide receiver James Lofton, and endured a slew of injuries throughout the regular season. Yet when it was over, the ever-resilient Bills were 12–4, atop the AFC East for the fifth time in six years, and again enjoying homefield advantage throughout the playoffs.

Buffalo won seven of its first eight games, including a dramatic and emotional 13–10 victory over the Cowboys in Dallas. There was a dip in the third quarter of the season, when the Bills dropped three of four, but they closed the schedule with a four-game, division-clinching winning streak that included a 47–34 conquest of the Dolphins in a nationally televised Sunday night game in Miami.

In December the Raiders had come to Buffalo and beaten the Bills 25–24, and when they returned a month later for a divisional-round playoff game, they almost pulled another shocker. They took a 17–6 second-quarter lead before Kelly threw a pair of touchdown passes to Bill Brooks, and Buffalo pulled out a 29–23 victory.

In the AFC Championship Game, Kansas City marched into Rich Stadium confident that its 23–7 shellacking of the Bills in November and the presence of its new quarterback, Joe Montana, would be enough to end Buffalo's reign in the AFC. Not even close. Montana was knocked out of the game with a concussion early in the third quarter, Thomas rushed for a Buffalo playoff record 186 yards and 3 touchdowns, and the Bills cruised to a 30–13 triumph to become the first team in history to reach the Super Bowl four consecutive years.

"I know we've won a lot of games in the 90s [fifty-eight to that point, including the postseason], but we still haven't won the one we want," said Levy.

And they never did.

Dallas was again the opponent for Super Bowl XXVIII at the Georgia Dome in Atlanta, and while the Bills didn't commit 9 turnovers, they did commit 3, including the one that turned the game around.

Each team kicked a field goal on its first possession, then Cowboys cornerback James Washington forced Thomas to

The Oh-for-Four Bunch

These twenty-three players dressed for all four of Buffalo's Super Bowl losses in the 1990s:

OT	Howard Ballard		CB	Nate Odomes
LB	Cornelius Bennett		OT	Glenn Parker
RB	Kenneth Davis		ST	Mark Pike
RB	Carwell Gardner		WR	Andre Reed
QB	Gale Gilbert		QB	Frank Reich
C	Kent Hull		OG	Jim Ritcher
QB	Jim Kelly		DE	Bruce Smith
FS	Mark Kelso		LB	Darryl Talley
LS	Adam Lingner		ST	Steve Tasker
DT	Mike Lodish		RB	Thurman Thomas
TE	Keith McKeller		NT	Jeff Wright
TE	Pete Metzelaars			

fumble at midfield, setting up a second Dallas field goal for a 6–3 lead. But when the Bills responded by driving 80 yards in 17 plays to Thomas's 4-yard touchdown run early in the second quarter, then tacked on a 28-yard field goal by Steve Christie on the final play of the half for a 13–6 lead, it looked as if Buffalo was primed to end its Super Bowl horror.

Alas, on the third play of the third quarter, the game turned irreversibly in Dallas's favor. Leon Lett forced a Thomas fumble, and Washington picked it up and raced 46 yards for the tying touchdown. Buffalo's spirit was crushed. On the next possession,

Emmitt Smith rammed the ball down the Bills' throats, eventually scoring on a 15-yard run, and in the fourth quarter, Washington picked off a Kelly pass in Buffalo territory to set up another Smith touchdown run that put the game away. The final tally was 30–13, and the Bills became the first pro sports team in history to lose its league championship game four straight times.

More than a decade has passed since that last Super Bowl loss to Dallas. As the years go by, the Bills seem to earn more and more respect from the football world for what they achieved in reaching four consecutive Super Bowls. But not from Levy. "I can't say that because I couldn't respect them any more than I've always respected them," he said. "This was as unique a group that has ever been put together. Sure, it hurts like the devil, for their sake, that we can't say we won one. I would have liked to have won them all—some of them, one of them—but we didn't, and you can't change it. But what they had to do to keep going back speaks such volumes for the type of character and resilience and closeness that they had, and still have. The last thing I want my players to feel is that their careers were somehow less significant because they didn't win a Super Bowl. There is something to be said for making it that close to the summit of the mountain four straight times."

←TICKETS
TICKETS
←

The Comeback

In the fall of 2004, former Bills receiver Don Beebe made his debut as a high school football coach in the suburbs of Chicago. In the third week of the season, his boys from Aurora Christian were preparing to play Chicago Christian, a team Aurora had never before beaten. Unlike his old Buffalo coach Marv Levy, who was a master at pregame speeches, Beebe wasn't sure what he was going to tell his players during the week of preparation for the big Private School League showdown. And then it came to him.

"One of the illustrations I used with the kids was the comeback game," Beebe said of the greatest game in Bills' history, in Buffalo sports history, and arguably in NFL history, Buffalo's unbelievable 41–38 overtime victory over the Houston Oilers in January 1993. In that AFC wild-card playoff game, the Bills rallied from a 35–3 third-quarter deficit to win.

"I told them it doesn't matter what the score is, it doesn't matter that we've never beaten this team before," Beebe continued. "I've been part of a game where we were down 35–3 in the third quarter, and we came back and won. As long as you keep hitting them and keep bringing it to them, you never know what the result is going to be until the final whistle."

Beebe's Eagles didn't need to pull off a miracle comeback. In a game that featured six lead changes, Aurora went ahead for good with nine minutes to play and held on to defeat Chicago Christian 42–33, ending the Knights seventeen-game league winning streak and their previous domination of Aurora.

"Just keep going at it, play as hard as you can," said Beebe. "You can live with the result if you do that, but if you don't try your best and you could have won and you didn't, that's unacceptable. That's what I'm trying to teach these kids, to have that never-give-up attitude."

It's an easy sell for Beebe because all his players have to do is remember the afternoon at Rich Stadium when their coach and the rest of his Buffalo teammates set the new standard on how to play to the final whistle, to never give up, and to try your best until the very end even if the scoreboard and the players on the other sideline are laughing at you.

Look it up, boys: The Bills were down 28–3 at halftime, then 35–3 two minutes into the third quarter after backup quarterback Frank Reich—playing in place of the injured Jim Kelly—threw an interception that was returned for a touchdown by Houston's Bubba McDowell. Yet there was Reich, even as the Oilers were lining up for the extra point in front of 75,141 Bills fans who were sitting in stunned and disappointed silence, imploring his team-mates to stay the course, to keep playing because, you know what, you never know.

"I remember Frank going up and down the sideline just saying, 'Hey, just keep making plays,'" Beebe said, a smile creeping across his face as he pictured the scene. "Frank never lost his perspective, he kept telling us to 'make plays, we're fine, just keep playing.' We weren't going to give up, that wasn't our mentality to do that, and he was right. We started making plays." And before long those plays resulted in the greatest comeback in NFL history, or, as Houston cornerback Cris Dishman prefers to call it, "the biggest choke in history."

"I told him before the second half, 'Well, Frank, you had the greatest comeback in college history, let's see if you can do it in the pros,' and he went out and did it," said Kelly. In 1984 Reich led his Maryland Terrapins back from a 31–0 halftime deficit to defeat the defending national champion, Miami, 42–40 in what was then the greatest comeback in college football history.

"In order to have a comeback like that, you have to make some big plays," said Kelly. "I'll tell you, the poise that Frank showed out there, I don't think it can be matched. That was the greatest win I've ever been associated with, and I was on the side-lines. It doesn't feel good standing there, but when a guy like Frank pulls through, that's great."

Quarterback Frank Reich engineered the big comeback against the Houston Oilers in their January 1993 playoff game.
Buffalo Bills

During the 1992 season the Bills were coming off back-to-back AFC championships as well as back-to-back Super Bowl defeats, and by the end of the regular season, it didn't look like they were going to get the opportunity to correct their Super Bowl deficiencies. By losing three of their last five games to finish with an 11–5 record, the Bills let the AFC East division title slip from their grasp for the first time in five years. Miami matched Buffalo's 11–5 record and won the tiebreaker based on a better record against AFC opponents after the Bills endured a 27–3 season-ending drubbing at the hands of the Oilers in the raucous Astrodome.

It was a gory night for the Bills because they were never competitive in the game. Compounding the ugliness, Kelly suffered a knee injury that would knock him out of action indefinitely. The loss to Houston forced the Bills into the wild-card playoff round the following week. While they would be at home at Rich Stadium where they had never lost a postseason game, they would have to play without their star quarterback against this same Houston team that clearly seemed to have Buffalo's number.

Thurman Thomas, Buffalo's star running back, tried to search for a positive thought to bring into the game. He settled on a scenario from 1990, when Kelly suffered a knee injury and Reich was called on to start the AFC East–deciding game against Miami. That day, Reich stepped in and guided the Bills to a 24–14 victory that began Buffalo's run to its first Super Bowl appearance.

Down in Houston the brash Oilers, who had talked some serious trash prior to their one-sided victory at the Astrodome, knew they would be in for a tougher game, even with Kelly on crutches watching from the bench. "A game like this helps our confidence," Dishman said of the Houston victory, "but we have to play the same way next time. In fact we have to play even better because we're playing in Buffalo."

For thirty-two minutes they played better than humanly possibly. Warren Moon completed 19 of his 22 first-half passes for 218 yards and 4 touchdowns as the Oilers gushed to a seemingly insurmountable 25-point lead. Beebe remembers sitting in front of his locker stall when special teams ace Steve Tasker leaned over and said, "Beebs, where are we playing golf next weekend?"

"It was said with thick sarcasm and disgust," Tasker said when recalling the moment. "I mean we weren't going golfing in January so it was a joke, but we were in pretty big trouble. I mean it was 28–3. But then we also said, 'Hey, we've been to two Super Bowls, we can't get embarrassed like this. Let's go out and battle in this second half so when they look back five years later in the media guide and see we got beat 28–17 or something, it won't look so bad. We've got to do that. Let's get some self-respect back.' "

But before self-respect there would be more embarrassment as Reich threw a pass to the right sideline that bounced off tight end Keith McKeller's hands and deflected right to McDowell, who sprinted untouched 58 yards to the end zone. At that point many fans in the crowd began packing their belongings and heading to the exits rather than watch their proud Bills get pummeled. In hindsight it seems as if the Oilers followed those folks right out to the parking lot.

"It was 35–3, but remember what happened the previous week," Reich said, pointing out the one-sided nature of Houston's 27–3 victory. "Now it's 62–6 over the last six quarters, so how could you not let up? I'm not saying they were weak-minded, but it would be hard not to let down a little bit after dominating a team for six quarters, and they did. Not a lot. It's not like they quit playing, but they opened the door just a little bit."

And the Bills came crashing through.

Backup running back Kenneth Davis—playing for Thomas, who was knocked out of the game with a hip injury just before McDowell's interception—capped a 50-yard drive by plunging over from the 1 to make it 35–10. "We took it in there and scored and it wasn't that hard, so maybe they did relax some," center Kent Hull said.

Steve Christie then successfully recovered his own surprise onside kick at Buffalo's 48 yard line, and 56 seconds later Reich lofted a 38-yard touchdown pass down the left sideline to Beebe. Now it was 35–17 and there was still half of the third quarter left to play. "I think after the touchdown I scored, I think that was the first time I came to the sidelines and guys were starting to think, 'Hey, let's keep this thing going,' " said Beebe.

To which Tasker agreed. "When Frank threw the interception and it was 35–3, everyone took a deep breath and said, 'Okay, let's finish it out strong,' " said Tasker. "But then the Oilers turned it off, and they were done. They just seemed to have no interest in playing the rest of that game. Bing, bing, bing, touchdown; surprise onside kick, bing, bing, bing, touchdown; and now it's 35–17, and we're like, 'Okay, we've got some self-respect, let's keep on playing.' "

After the Oilers went three and out, a poor 25-yard Greg Montgomery punt gave the Bills the ball at their own 41 yard line. Four plays later, Reich threaded a perfect strike to Andre Reed over the middle for a 26-yard touchdown. Suddenly, it was 35–24. "When we scored to make it 35–24 late in the third quarter, that's when I thought it was really within reach," Reich

The Box Score

Bills 41, Oilers 38 (OT)

Oilers	7	21	7	3	0	—	38
Bills	3	0	28	7	3	—	41

First Quarter

Hou—Jeffires 3 pass from Moon (Del Greco kick), 9:09 elapsed.

Buf—FG Christie 36, 13:36.

Second Quarter

Hou—Slaughter 7 pass from Moon (Del Greco kick), 6:01.

Hou—Duncan 26 pass from Moon (Del Greco kick), 10:51.

Hou—Jeffires 27 pass from Moon (Del Greco kick), 14:46.

Third Quarter

Hou—McDowell 58 interception return (Del Greco kick), 1:41.

Buf—K. Davis 1 run (Christie kick), 6:08.

Buf—Beebe 38 pass from Reich (Christie kick), 7:04.

Buf—Reed 26 pass from Reich (Christie kick), 10:19.

Buf—Reed 18 pass from Reich (Christie kick), 13:00.

Fourth Quarter

Buf—Reed 17 pass from Reich (Christie kick), 11:52.

Hou—FG Del Greco 26, 14:48.

Overtime

Buf—FG Christie 32, 3:06.

Attendance—75,141.

Team Statistics	Bills	Oilers
First downs	19	27
Rushing yards	98	82
Passing yards	268	347
Punts–avg	2-35.0	2-24.5
Fumbles–lost	0-0	2-0
Penalties–yards	4–30	4–30
Possession time	25:27	37:39

said. "If the defense just kept playing the way they were playing and the offense kept executing, there was plenty of time."

Sure enough, the defense continued its miraculous recovery as Henry Jones picked off a Moon pass and brought it back to Houston's 23 yard line. After two Davis runs for 5 yards and an incompletion, the Bills were faced with fourth and 5 at the 18. Following a timeout, Coach Marv Levy eschewed the field goal. The bold move paid off when Reich fired a touchdown pass to Reed. There were still two minutes remaining in the third quarter, and the Bills were within four at 35–31.

"The Oilers couldn't turn it back on," said Tasker. "When Frank hit Andre to make it 35–31, that game was over, and we were still down by four. We knew we were going to beat them. That fourth-down throw to Andre, it was over. We couldn't stop, we were on fire, the defense was on fire, and the crowd was insane."

After an exchange of punts, Houston drove from its own 10 yard line to Buffalo's 14. It looked as if the Bills might be running out of energy, having expended so much just to get back into the game. Instead, the defense stiffened and forced a field-goal attempt. When the holder, Montgomery, muffed the snap to abort the kick, the Bills took possession at their own 26 with a chance to take the lead.

Seven plays later, that mission was accomplished. After Davis scampered 35 yards to convert a crucial third and four, Reich and Reed hooked up for their third touchdown, this time a 17-yarder that put the Bills up 38–35 with 3:08 to play.

Somehow, the Oilers regrouped long enough for Moon to march them 63 yards to Al Del Greco's overtime-forcing 26-yard field goal with 12 seconds to go, and when Houston won the coin

What They Said

Here are some of the postgame comments after the Bills' historic come-from-behind victory over the Oilers in a 1993 AFC wild-card playoff game:

- Bills linebacker Darryl Talley: "Believe, believe, believe. What this shows is that this team has a helluva lot of character."

- Bills running back Kenneth Davis: "I've never seen anything wilder than this. When we won the AFC championship [51–3 over the Raiders in 1990] on the way to the first Super Bowl, it wasn't this great. This was a very emotional win for us."

- Bills wide receiver Andre Reed: "Of course, it seemed like it was hopeless. Our defense wasn't stopping them. It seemed like they were going to run up and down the field all day on us. But I guess the Oilers got a little lackadaisical out there, and it gave us a chance to get the momentum."

- Bills quarterback Frank Reich: "Without question, it's the game of my life. I was pretty emotional when I got back to the locker room. I couldn't hold the tears back."

- Bills coach Marv Levy on Reich: "Frank is a person of high character. He's a well-rounded family man who's deeply religious. Sometimes the guy who has other things in his life doesn't clutch up. It makes him be able to retain an equilibrium."

- Levy on his thoughts at halftime: "I was just thinking this is a humiliating day. Did I still think we had a chance? Well, there was a lot of time left so there was a glimmer of hope, but it was about the same chance as you have of winning the New York lottery."

- Oilers cornerback Cris Dishman: "It was the biggest choke in history . . . We were outplayed and outcoached in the second half. When we had them down, we should have cut their throats, but we let them breathe and gave them new life. Never in my wildest nightmares did I believe something like this could happen."

- Oilers wide receiver Ernest Givins: "It's like somebody, somewhere, has a voodoo doll, and when the Houston Oilers go on the road to play a playoff game, they start sticking pins in the voodoo doll until there's nothing left of the Houston Oilers."

toss to start the extra period, there was a glimmer of nervousness in the crowd. The Oilers had shown some heart on their final drive, they had some momentum, and now they had the ball first in a sudden-death situation. Bills fans couldn't help but think of the gruesome possibility that all that work, all that drama, all that courage in the face of overwhelming odds was going to go for naught.

Not on this historic day. Not this game for the ages.

On the third play of overtime, Buffalo cornerback Nate Odomes intercepted a poorly thrown Moon pass and returned it to the Oilers 20. After two Davis plunges, Levy sent Christie onto the field to attempt a 32-yard field goal on third down. There wasn't a breath being drawn in the moments before Christie whipped his right leg through the hold of Reich, but then a hurricane of unbridled joy blew through the stadium as the ball soared on a perfect path between the uprights, ending the game that redefined the art of the comeback.

Nose tackle Jeff Wright summed up the amazement of both teams over what transpired when he shared a postgame moment spent with Houston defensive end Ray Childress. "He said to me, 'I've never seen anything like this,' and his eyes were like bugged out," Wright recalled. "I told him, 'Me neither.' "

Reich recognizes his role in the comeback, and he knows that his 289-yard, four-touchdown performance that day will forever be etched in NFL lore. But what he enjoyed most about that game is that he did not march alone on that path to glory. "That game was a huge high, it was a mountain-top experience, it was being in the zone, it was all those things you hear, all those athletic metaphors that we use," he said. "But what was so fun about it, and what really hasn't changed, is what made it so special. It was that you shared it with your teammates. This is a team game, and so much of what my life has been about and the way I was brought up with my parents being coaches and teachers and emphasizing team, team, team, was reflected in that game. That game epitomizes a team effort to come back."

In the days and weeks after the game, the Bills received congratulatory messages from all corners of the globe. People who were dying of cancer sent letters saying the Bills' comeback had inspired them to fight harder. Teachers sent letters explaining how the Bills' comeback would become a teaching aide for them. Tasker was touched by so many of the well-wishers, but the one piece of mail that he felt symbolized best what the Bills had done came from a member of the U.S. Marine Corps.

"It was a drawing of a pelican with a frog in its mouth," Tasker recalled with a laugh. "The frog was reaching out of the pelican's mouth and gripping its throat so the pelican couldn't swallow, and it said, 'Never give up.' In our part of the country, that game is like, 'Where were you when JFK was shot?' But it's, 'Where were you when the Bills came back to beat the Oilers?' "

The Mother of All Quarterback Controversies

It was the afternoon of January 3, 2000, and I was among a throng of reporters gathered in the Buffalo Bills media room covering coach Wade Phillips's weekly Monday press conference. These sessions were usually reserved for reviewing with the media what had transpired in the previous day's game. Then Phillips would answer questions about the Bills upcoming opponent.

So there we stood, me and my fellow newspaper, television, and radio colleagues, fixated on

Phillips as he was about to recount—or so we thought—how his Bills had shredded the Indianapolis Colts, 31–6, in the regular-season finale at Ralph Wilson Stadium. But first, Phillips had a little announcement to make. Rob Johnson, who had started exactly one game all year—that victory twenty-four hours earlier over the Colts—would be Buffalo's starting quarterback six days hence for the Bills wild-card playoff game in Tennessee instead of Doug Flutie.

Stunned silence. Blank stares transformed into wide-eyed looks of disbelief. As the words were spilling out of Phillips's mouth, neither I nor anyone else present could believe what we were hearing. Needless to say, once we regained our wits and what Phillips had said registered in our brains, there wasn't much conversation about that Colts game or even about the playoff matchup with the Titans.

Flutie had started the first fifteen games and posted a 10–5 record. While his performance hadn't been nearly as impressive as in 1998, when he earned a Pro Bowl invitation and was named the NFL's comeback player of the year, he had still guided the Bills into the playoffs for the second consecutive year.

Johnson, we were told, had only been tabbed to start against the Colts so that Flutie could rest his thirty-seven-year-old body before having to face the Titans. Sure, Johnson had played fabulously, completing 24 of 32 passes for 287 yards and 2 touchdowns without being sacked. But it came against a Colts team whose main focus was getting out of the game healthy because it was already locked in as the number-two seed in the AFC playoffs.

It was one game, a rather meaningless one at that, played by a guy who had been encased in mothballs all season. Now, with the biggest game of the year on the horizon, Phillips was willing

Rob Johnson became Buffalo's starting quarterback after defeating the Indianapolis Colts. Buffalo Bills

to turn the team over to Johnson based on that one performance. It seemed foolhardy, ludicrous, bordering on irresponsible. Robert Hicks, the Bills mammoth 350-pound offensive right tackle that season, summed up best the surprise that players, coaches, reporters, and fans throughout western New York felt when he said, "You could have knocked me over with a feather when I heard, and that's saying a lot considering how big I am."

It was on that day that the Flutie-Johnson quarterback controversy, a simmering dispute during their first two years together with the Bills, grew fangs and became a monster that divided the team until the spring of 2001, when new general manager Tom Donahoe closed that ignominious chapter in team history by releasing Flutie.

The NFL has seen its share of quarterback controversies. Three of the most famous were Joe Montana and Steve Young in San Francisco, Craig Morton and Roger Staubach in Dallas, and Sonny Jurgensen and Billy Kilmer in Washington, but there have been dozens of others through the decades. Few, if any, became as mean-spirited and damaging to the team as Flutie-Johnson. My colleague at the *Democrat and Chronicle*, Leo Roth, once wrote that "Flutie and Johnson was Bill Clinton and Monica Lewinsky in helmets."

Johnson, on the day in March 2001 when he learned that Donahoe and new coach Gregg Williams had decided to keep him and waive Flutie, said: "I wish you guys [the media] knew the total situation of how divided the team was and how mentally draining it can be. I mean coaches were taking sides, it was that bad. Guys would come out of meetings and they'd say things like, 'Boy, they really bad-mouthed you and they're rooting for the other guy.' And it was vice versa for Doug. It just wore on me. Three years is tough to deal with."

The genesis of the controversy occurred in 1997, when Buffalo quarterback Todd Collins proved to the world that he was capable of nothing more than carrying a clipboard on an NFL sideline. Jim Kelly had retired following the 1996 season and his heir apparent, Collins, a former second-round Buffalo draft choice, flopped miserably as Kelly's replacement. The Bills skidded to a 6–10 record, their worst since a 4–12 mark in Kelly's rookie season of 1986.

Realizing that Collins was not the answer, the Bills brain-trust—led by general manager John Butler, Phillips, and pro-personnel director A. J. Smith—began an exhaustive quarterback search. With a weak crop of free agents about to hit the market, the Bills went the unconventional route: They aimed their sights north of the border to the Canadian Football League and lured Flutie back to the NFL.

"I knew his contract would expire [at the end of 1997] so that's when I started tracking him," said Smith, who provided the primary impetus for the signing. "I think he's a winner and a football player. I don't care about his size. People say it's a detriment, but the way the league has changed, you need to have a mobile quarterback. I like his instincts for the game, he pulls the trigger quickly, and he's one of the greatest competitors I've ever seen in any league at any time. I'm sure glad he's on the Buffalo Bills."

Flutie, the 1984 Heisman Trophy winner from Boston College, had been unable to make it in the NFL during his first five years as a pro, so he took his entertaining brand of football up to Canada. There he enjoyed a remarkably successful eight-year stint—some would call it an exile—in the CFL, earning six MVP awards and winning four Grey Cup championships.

The Original Quarterback Controversy

The Doug Flutie-Rob Johnson quarterback controversy wasn't the first to split the Bills in half. Back in the Bills' heyday in the mid-1960s, when they were winning back-to-back AFL championships, Jack Kemp and Daryle Lamonica spent time jockeying back and forth at the position.

Kemp came to Buffalo in 1962 via a waiver transaction from San Diego, and he immediately solidified a position that had been a major weakness in Buffalo. Lamonica arrived in 1963 as a twenty-fourth-round draft pick out of Notre Dame and provided Kemp with all the push he needed. Throughout the championship years of 1964 and 1965, Lamonica would often relieve an ineffective Kemp, and coach Lou Saban even started Lamonica on occasion.

However, their relationship was never frosty, and Kemp—who was often serenaded with the chant "We Want Lamonica" by the hard-to-please Buffalo fans—said it always bothered him that the fans and media tried to portray him and Lamonica as bitter rivals who didn't like each other. "We were certainly rivals and competitors, and I can't say that we were as close as we are today," said Kemp. "It wasn't mean-spirited, but it was certainly competitive, and I think competitiveness brings out the best in everybody. I could not understand why some fans could not accept the fact that every team needs not one but two quarterbacks."

Lamonica, who was traded to the Oakland Raiders before the 1967 season and led them to the 1967 AFL championship and a berth in Super Bowl II, said he appreciated his time with Kemp. "I learned from Jack as his backup," he said. "Jack and I were always very close. He was my tutor."

He had yearned for a return to the NFL, if for no other reason than to prove that the Chicago Bears and hometown New England Patriots had been wrong about him, and that he could be a productive and winning quarterback in the league. For about three weeks Flutie thought he was going to get that opportunity as he seemed set as the Bills starting quarterback with only Collins, Alex Van Pelt, and Jim Ballard to beat out. But then Butler pulled the trigger on a high-profile trade that had Flutie shaking his head in disbelief and anger. Butler sent the Bills first-round position in the upcoming 1998 draft (number nine overall) plus their fourth-round spot to Jacksonville for Johnson, Mark Brunell's backup the previous three years.

Though Johnson had played very little since joining the Jaguars from USC as a fourth-round draft pick in 1995, he put on a clinic in his only NFL start when he passed for 294 yards against the Baltimore Ravens in a 1997 game. With his ideal size (6' 4", 215 pounds), athletic ability, and strong arm, not to mention the fact that he was eleven years younger than Flutie, the Bills saw Johnson as their quarterback of the future.

Flutie couldn't help but feel betrayed by this development, and the chip he carried on his shoulder grew to the size of a boulder. Still, he soldiered on during the off-season and into training camp and seemed to form a workable relationship with Johnson. Buffalo's first game in 1998 was in San Diego, and the Chargers provided Bills fans with a glimpse of what was to come over the next four years. They sacked Johnson 5 times and knocked him out of the game early in the third quarter. Flutie came in and threw 2 touchdown passes to Andre Reed to put the Bills ahead 14–13. After the Chargers regained the lead on a John Carney field goal, Flutie drove the Bills into position to win the game, only to have Steve Christie miss a 39-yard field goal with 3 seconds left.

Johnson returned to action, and the Bills lost their next two games to Miami and St. Louis before Johnson pulled himself together and played wonderfully in a 26–21 upset of San Francisco. After that game it looked as if Johnson was finally comfortable in his role as the starter. He had almost four games under his belt, and the Bills were confident that he would lead them back into playoff contention.

But in week 5 Buffalo traveled to Indianapolis. While getting sacked on the third play of the game, Johnson fell awkwardly on the point of the ball and tore cartilage in his rib cage. Originally it was thought he'd miss a game or two and then he'd take back the job. Instead, Johnson watched Flutie steal his job by playing excellent, exciting, and winning football, while captivating Buffalo fandom and giving birth to a new cereal product, Flutie Flakes, in the process. Flutie, not Johnson, drove the Bills to the playoffs.

Flutie completed 23 of 28 passes for 213 yards and 2 touchdowns after replacing Johnson in Indianapolis, and the Bills beat the Colts. In his first start against unbeaten Jacksonville in week 6, Flutie scrambled around left end on an improvised bootleg for the winning touchdown with 13 seconds remaining, and a love affair between Flutie and Bills fans was hatched. Little Dougie became the workingman's hero, while Johnson was portrayed as the southern California surfer dude without a soul.

As Johnson sat and recuperated, Flutie led the Bills to seven wins in ten starts. By the time the season finale was played, the Bills had clinched a wild-card playoff berth. With nothing on the line, Phillips played Johnson against New Orleans. He was very sharp in a 45–33 victory, but Flutie was the man under center

Doug Flutie became a fan favorite in Buffalo. Buffalo Bills

when the Bills went to Miami for the wild-card game the following week.

With Flutie throwing for 360 yards against Miami's very talented defense, the Bills nearly pulled the upset. However, trailing 24–17 with five seconds left to play and the Bills at the Dolphins 5 yard line, Flutie was sacked and lost a fumble, and the Bills season came to an end.

Based on Flutie's performance in 1998, there was no controversy in 1999. He was the starter and Johnson was the backup, though there were some grumblings around town from Johnson supporters who recognized that Flutie wasn't nearly as effective as he had been the season before. Despite his declining play, Flutie still led the Bills to a 10–5 record and another playoff berth.

That should have been enough to guarantee him the start in Tennessee for the wild-card game, regardless of what Johnson did in the season finale against the Colts. Phillips didn't see it that way. Mesmerized by Johnson's clinic against the Colts, and perhaps pushed by team owner Ralph Wilson to play the man whom Wilson was paying an average of $5 million per year, Phillips floored the entire football nation by designating Johnson as the starter against the Titans.

"I think the team feels like we can win with either one of them," Phillips explained. "It's a tough decision, certainly, but it's something you look at objectively. I studied the film, it wasn't a haphazard thing. I talked to our coaches, and I think it gives us the best opportunity to win this game. And I think our team has confidence in Rob. If they didn't, I wouldn't have made the change."

Flutie was furious. He said all the right things to the media, but privately he stewed over this breach of faith, and his already strained relationship with Johnson became untenable from then on.

Johnson played well enough to lift the Bills into a 16–15 lead in the final moments against the Titans, but then Buffalo surrendered the ghastly "Music City Miracle" kickoff return—a crossfield lateral that was returned for a touchdown in the closing seconds—and Tennessee escaped with an unfathomable 22–16 victory.

"That Tennessee thing was much more than a bloop kick and a runback," said Steve Christie, hinting that the quarterback controversy was too much for the Bills to deal with. "Half the locker room was on one side and the others were on the other side. That's no way to go into the playoffs. You can't point blame one way or the other. It's just the players were confused. You need to be a solid unit, mentally and physically, going into the playoffs, and I don't think we were."

It only got worse in 2000. During that winter Flutie told a Canadian television station that he felt the Bills would have beaten Tennessee if he had been quarterback. Johnson fired back in an interview in *Penthouse* magazine saying that Flutie wasn't much fun to play with.

Phillips declared an open battle for the quarterback position in training camp, and while that may have been good from a competitive standpoint, it further drove a wedge into the team. Some players and coaches were Johnson backers, others were Flutie fanatics. The media seemed to support Johnson, but the fans were clearly on Flutie's side. In other words Buffalo in the fall of 2000 was like an active volcano, ready to erupt at any moment.

"The guys are divided because everyone likes Rob, he's a good guy and he's laid back," said Christie. "But Doug gets them going much more when he's on the field. He changes things when he's out there. It's a different game with Doug."

Johnson was awarded the starting job for the opener, a rematch with the Titans in Orchard Park, but it was an easy call for Phillips because Flutie had suffered a groin injury in camp and could not play the first month of the season. Against Tennessee, it was typical Johnson as an ankle injury knocked him out of the game. Thus, it was Alex Van Pelt, the third-string quarterback, who entered and drove the Bills to a game-winning field goal.

Johnson rebounded with an excellent performance in beating Brett Favre and Green Bay, but then he hit the skids during a three-game losing streak against AFC East rivals New York, Indianapolis, and Miami. He set career highs for completions, attempts, and passing yards in a victory over San Diego, but once again he did not finish the job. He hurt his shoulder in overtime, and guess who came to the rescue? Flutie, healthy again, marched the Bills into position for Christie's winning field goal.

Johnson sat out the next four games, and in typical fashion Flutie took advantage of his foil's absence. He played heroically in a loss at Minnesota, then directed victories over the Jets, Patriots, and Bears. But Phillips had said all along that Johnson was his quarterback, and when he was healthy enough to play, he would. So despite the three-game winning streak with Flutie at the helm, Johnson was named the starter for Buffalo's game at Kansas City.

At this point nerves were frayed, allegiances became even more defined, and when the two quarterbacks began sniping at each other in public, all hell began to break loose. In a *Sports Illustrated* article, unnamed players were quoted regarding the quarterback issue. One said, "There's no question we're a different team with Doug in there. All Doug thinks about is helping the team win and how he can do that. Rob seems distracted by things like wanting everyone to like him."

Johnson read the story and sincerely believed that the anonymous quote came from none other than Flutie, and he confronted Flutie. "I asked him about it, and I was pretty ticked off," said Johnson. Flutie denied any wrongdoing, but the two barely spoke to each other the rest of the season.

Oh yes, the season. Johnson returned against the Chiefs and directed a gritty 21–17 victory in Kansas City, scoring the winning touchdown on a 12-yard run in the final three minutes. It looked as if it might be a defining moment in his career, the day he took the job once and for all and relegated Flutie to the bench. Instead, the Bills lost their next four games to fall out of playoff contention, and in every game Flutie saw relief time in place of Johnson. The final occurrence came against New England, when Johnson was knocked out with a concussion, and Flutie nearly led the Bills to victory before losing in overtime. Flutie then started the season finale in Seattle and passed for 366 yards and 3 touchdowns in a 42–23 victory.

"It was just weird, man," said defensive end Marcellus Wiley of that 2000 season. "It was totally *The Young and the Restless.*"

The week of the Seattle game, Butler was fired by Wilson, and in the days after that game, Phillips and almost all of his coaching staff were axed. Meanwhile, Johnson and Flutie were still bitter teammates, but that too-long-running soap opera mercifully was about to end.

When the new general manager Tom Donahoe and head coach Gregg Williams rode into town proclaiming they would resurrect the Bills, they studied the quarterback situation in depth and announced that one was staying and one was going. Flutie seemed to have the inside track because Donahoe, who was out of football during 2000 after being fired from the Pittsburgh

Tale of the Tape

Here is a statistical comparison between quarterbacks Doug Flutie and Rob Johnson during their Buffalo careers:

	Flutie	Johnson
Games	39	30
Games started	30	26
Record	21–9	9–17
Completions	598	401
Attempts	1,063	663
Pct complete	56.2	60.4
Passing yards	7,582	4,798
Touchdowns	47	27
Interceptions	30	17
Rushing attempts	172	110
Rushing yards	876	746
Rushing avg	5.1	6.8
Rushing TDs	3	3

Steelers, had said while working that year for ESPN.com about the turmoil in Buffalo: "Flutie is 21–9 as the starter. What's the decision?"

Well, Donahoe certainly changed his tune. Both Flutie and Johnson were brought in for separate interviews and workouts, and in the end, Johnson (8–10 as a starter for the Bills to that point) was the choice. Flutie was sent packing.

"We took a month to make the decision," said Williams, who after three lackluster years was fired following the 2003 season and replaced by current coach Mike Mularkey. "We looked at every play each of them was involved in. We interviewed everyone who ever coached them in college, in the Canadian league, and in the NFL. Then we interviewed them both. It was probably the first job interview either of them ever had. We took a full day with each of them. I felt there was no way we could make that decision without doing that."

Williams was asked if, during their deliberation, was keeping both ever an option? No way, he said. "They hated each other," Williams acknowledged. "You like to have two quarterbacks who can both play, but you couldn't have that situation."

Johnson was thrilled to be the "winner" and expressed great relief that Flutie was out of his life. "We just didn't see eye to eye from the first day. I just think we're very different guys." As for Flutie, he didn't leave town without taking a couple more shots. "The only thing that really ticked me off is the perception that Rob beat me out, that he's better than me. If they truly believe Rob is the best guy for the job, then I have no problem with that. But shouldn't winning games account for something?"

Butler was hired to run the operation in San Diego, and he quickly signed Flutie to be his quarterback. Wiley also left Buffalo via free agency and joined the Chargers, and he weighed in one last time on the controversy. "All I know is we won more games with Doug [in Buffalo]," said Wiley. "Doug had more support. If you had to take a vote, Doug's going to win that one. It's not because of who's taller, who's older. All those things are secondary to who won more games."

With the job to himself in 2001 Johnson, predictably, failed. Playing on a team that had been gutted by the salary cap and free agency, Johnson was unable to provide a spark. The Bills won just one of their first eight games with Johnson as the starter, with one of the losses coming in San Diego, when Flutie exacted the sweetest revenge on Johnson and the Bills by scoring the winning touchdown on a 13-yard scramble with 1:10 left to play.

Johnson's season came to an end in the eighth game, against New England, when he suffered a broken clavicle. That turned out to be the last game he would play for the Bills. Prior to the start of the 2002 free-agency period, Johnson refused to take a pay cut that would have saved the Bills some salary cap space, so Donahoe released him. That was the best thing Johnson ever did for the Bills, because without his salary on the payroll, funds were freed up that enabled the Bills to get quarterback Drew Bledsoe in a trade with the Patriots.

Not that life was any better in Buffalo with Bledsoe under center. After a dazzling first half of 2002 that had all of western New York forgetting about the controversial last four years, Bledsoe hit the wall and was nearly as disappointing as Johnson during his three-year tenure in Buffalo. Bledsoe managed just a 23–25 record as a starter before being released following the 2004 season. The only difference is that at least the Bills knew who their quarterback was every week, and there was no locker room dissension despite the team's struggles.